MW01517281

New Country, New Life

A FAMILY MEMOIR

Chrystyna Holman

By

Chrystyna Zorych Holman

◆ FriesenPress

One Printers Way
Altona, MB R0G 0B0
Canada

www.friesenpress.com

Copyright © 2023 by Chrystyna Zorych Holman
First Edition — 2023

Bookmark - workmanship by Chrystyna Holman. Ukrainian embroidery, pattern from the region of Bukovyna, Western Ukraine. After centuries of enslavement, Ukrainian embroidery became: (Arey 1977)

an important factor in the national rebirth that the 19th century brought to Ukraine: along with the Ukrainian language and song, Ukrainian embroidery nourished the national consciousness of the Ukrainian masses.

All rights reserved.

No part of this publication may be reproduced in any form, or by any means, electronic or mechanical, including photocopying, recording, or any information browsing, storage, or retrieval system, without permission in writing from FriesenPress.

ISBN
978-1-03-918424-4 (Hardcover)
978-1-03-918423-7 (Paperback)
978-1-03-918425-1 (eBook)

1. BIOGRAPHY & AUTOBIOGRAPHY, PERSONAL MEMOIRS

Distributed to the trade by The Ingram Book Company

Table of Contents

Mr. Zorycz Bohdan
born 30 VIII 1912
at Sianik
State Stateless

is employed as singer in the choir
„Dumka".
The choir existed with consens
Military Gouvernment

Chairman

Choir „Dumka"
Innsbruck Tyrol

Certificate

Nr. 14

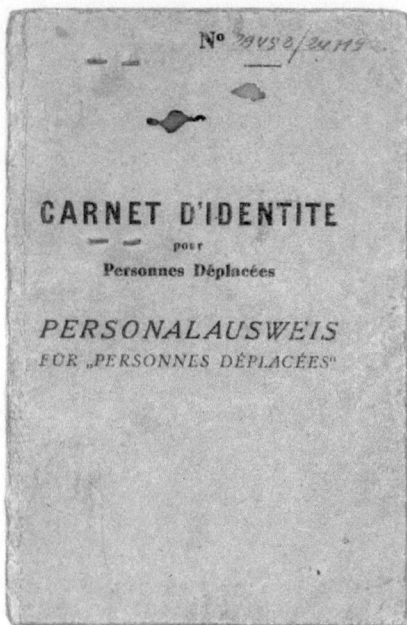

Emprentes digitales

Signature: J. Zorycz

NOM et prénom usuel
Name und Vorname
Z O R Y C Z
Jaroslawa

Taille 160   Corpulence   moyenne
Grösse   *Gestalt*

Cheveux blonds f. Yeux bleus
Haarfarbe   *Augenfarbe*

Signes particuliers — *Besondere Kennzeichen*

néant

A1   Délivré à   Feldkirch

No 2492/24719
A 1

HAUT COMMISSARIAT
DE LA RÉPUBLIQUE FRANÇAISE
EN AUTRICHE

MISSION DE CONTRÔLE-SECTION P.D.R.

Bezirk de   Feldkirch

NOM   Z O R Y C Z
NAME

Prénoms   Jaroslawa
Vorname

Né le 17.2.1917 à Belaniwice
geboren am   *in*

Galicie, Autriche

Nationalité à la naissance   autrichienne
Staatsangehörigkeit bei der Geburt

Nationalité au 1.9.1939   polonaise
Staatsangehörigkeit am 1.9.1939

Nationalité actuelle   polonaise (Ukrain.)
Derzeitige Staatsangehörigkeit

No 2492/24719

CARNET D'IDENTITE
pour
Personnes Déplacées

PERSONALAUSWEIS
FÜR „PERSONNES DÉPLACÉES"

Acknowledgements

This book came about from my storytelling. Telling a story is very different than writing it. I never felt competent to actually write down the history of my family's exile from their homeland and survival in Canada. Nonetheless, it's important that my children and grandchildren know their origins, where they came from and what brought them here. To respect the families of the people I am writing about, I have in some cases used initials or changed names of people no longer with us.

There are sad passages and there is humour, and above all, Ukrainian refugees had a tremendous commitment to help each other and their community to survive.

In writing this memoir, my friends supported and encouraged me. Some were anxious to see this writing effort in print. Most have heard the happy bits, the stories that are entertaining, but everyone knew that was not all there would be in this work. There are difficult passages spread throughout the various pages.

I owe endless thanks to the following people ....

Louise Polland is the editor who has sat in my kitchen for hours, carefully going through pages of type and giving me sensible suggestions. Louise has a talent which makes one think that the improvements she creates are basically your own ideas. It's a clever technique, and it is so typical of Louise not to take any credit. Humble to a fault, she cuts and pastes a little here, a little there, and the lines come to life. The Italian phrase grazie mille comes to mind.

Nollaig Bonar is a computer whiz and has pulled this work together and made it print-ready. Generous, talented, and amazing—that is who she is. She has spent hours and hours coming to my assistance. When my computer died and I lost all my written stories, Nollaig was able to recover what I had lost. All I know is that the computer experts could not retrieve the stories, but Nollaig was able to produce a printed copy of my work.

Regardless of how often I needed help, Nollaig would come and sort it all out. I simply do not know how to thank Nollaig for her magnanimity and her remarkably good humour.

Kvitka, my eldest daughter, read this book and concluded that the ending was too sad. It occurred to me that perhaps my children's memories would ease the harsh ending. All three wrote a few paragraphs, which I think end this book in the best way. So to Kvitka, Larissa, and Zoja, your mother is grateful and appreciates your sentiments and efforts.

To get this book ready for the world, Larissa offered to help with the layout and worked through the final corrections. Maria Malanchuk, an expert of Ukrainian history, literature, and culture, helped to oversee the content—especially as it related to Ukraine. It was so generous of her to give me the attention I needed.

Maria and I grew up together, and she is well-acquainted with the people I wrote about. She would often jog my memory and remind me of something I might have overlooked or forgotten. For all those recollections, I am very grateful.

Brenda Brady is my sister-in-law, and I don't know how to thank her. I am very grateful that she worked closely with me, rearranging sections of the book to ensure it had a logical progression. Brenda gave me hours of her time, sharing her expertise in proper English usage and her excellent computer skills.

I also want to thank Marta Olynyk, a transliterator of Ukrainian words to English. Marta's help was invaluable in correcting my efforts at transliteration.

Although not part of the editorial team, I would like to thank my husband. I liked to work on this project at the kitchen table. I needed the space and the light. It just felt good to work on this in my kitchen and close to the coffee pot. Alan never once complained about the mess and all those piles of paper on our kitchen table. He also never complained when I lost track of the time, and would suggest, "Eggs OK tonight?" Dinner was never expected on time, and that made life easier.

The photos in this book are the contributions of my sister Kvitka Kondracki. Larysa Hwozdulych, my childhood friend, contributed a very special photo, for which I am very grateful. Photographs make a difference. They help to put a face to a name. Thank you both.

In closing, I just want to say that life worked out for us here, in Canada. For this, I give credit to my parents—their determination to lead a decent life and to be responsible and caring citizens, because this is what we owe the country that gave us hope.

Preface

These stories are my memories. They begin in Austria and carry on through our life in Canada. I wrote them down because my parents' history reflects their will to survive. Theirs was a life well lived, full of purpose.

I want my children and my grandchildren to know who their grandparents/great-grandparents were. I also wish to pay tribute to their extraordinary lives. My parents were not saints, but they were decent, community-minded, generous, and altruistic. Both of them were writers, and my mother was a well-established editor in the Ukrainian language.

Life with them was not only interesting and entertaining but could also be difficult at times. This too is documented. Their hardships were many but they did manage to bring my sister and me to freedom and safety.

Both my parents had a remarkable sense of humour, which carried them through tough times as they tried to establish a life in Canada. Being children of very patriotic citizens, loyal to their former homeland as well as to their new country, made life a trial for us at times.

These are the memories of a young child and at the end of the day, these are my recollections. This book is written, as best as possible, in chronological order. However, I deviate at times in order to explain or provide a clearer picture of an event.

Writing down my parents' history is something I have always wanted to do, but it took an unusual amount of time to get started. I have tried to present most of the stories with a humorous touch. It is the extremes in life that one remembers best.

My sister and I pose for an ad requesting Ukrainians in the Western world to help
Ukrainian refugees. For this picture, we wore our best outfits. Mrs. B made the
dresses. Both the dresses and the stockings look smart, but they were pure wool,
and they itched and scratched.

Survival

My parents did not talk about the Second World War or about their escape from Ukraine to freedom. They are gone now, and I am sorry that I did not push a little harder to have that piece of their history. I know bits and pieces of what I heard—or more likely overheard. Conversations that were not meant for my ears. There are a few memories, quite sketchy, not at all clear, of how we managed to leave Ukraine and end up in Canada.

I am not a historian, and not in a position to explain my parents' realities, so I write this based on the few stories they told. I do know that my father was in the Resistance and my mother was involved in the movement. They met at a political rally and their relationship began with a common goal: an independent and free Ukraine.

When the war broke out, my mother was in Lviv, and realised that she had to get home to her small village in Western Ukraine. She tried to get on the train, but it was packed, the doors were shut, the train was ready to go. A couple of young fellows on the train realised her dilemma and opened the window and said, "Miss, do you need to get on this train?" Of course, she needed to get on the train! They pulled her in through the window.

She had to get home to see her parents and ensure they were OK. I understood that the train ride took her to safety. Home was where she knew all the villagers—and knew they would hide her, if necessary.

The Allies were quite aware of the Resistance movement in Western Ukraine. They knew that Hitler had promised to create an independent and free Ukraine and that Ukrainians had sided with the Nazis in the beginning, naïvely believing him. It did not take long to realise that Hitler would not deliver on his promise, but wanted to use the country as a base to advance upon Russia. So people like my parents found themselves hunted by the

Polish and Russian forces, as both countries were part of the Allied forces, and eventually by the Nazis.

Both Russia and Poland had a vested interest in controlling Ukraine. The black, rich soil of the steppes was considered the breadbasket of Europe. Moreover, Eastern Ukraine had oil, gas, coal, uranium, and other minerals and fossil fuels.

The history of that time is far more complicated, but it explains why my parents' escape was difficult. The first thing I remember my mother telling me was that not long after she got home, Polish soldiers came to arrest her because she was a member of the Ukrainian Resistance. She had left Lviv, so the village was the next place to look for her. News of Polish soldiers advancing toward her village caused her to take cover. She hid in the neighbour's barn in the loft, over the high rafters, where she was well concealed but had a tiny peephole to watch the soldiers' actions. She was afraid that the soldiers would take her father, a priest, if they could not find her, and she would not allow that.

They looked in every corner of the house and in every barrel near the house, which contained food crops from the harvest. She watched the bayonets thrust into straw piles to make sure she was not there. They were about to arrest her father when one of the maids rang the church bells. The village woke up. People came running and surrounded the few soldiers and my grandfather. One of the villagers said, "You take our priest; you take us all!" The soldiers left. They couldn't arrest the whole village, and they couldn't shoot them all. There were too many of them, so the saying that there is safety in numbers proved to be true in this case.

Months later, it was the Russians who appeared, but just as they were about to arrest my grandfather, word was received that the German forces were closing in on the village, and the soldiers fled.

After my sister's birth, my mother realised that she had to leave the country where she had been born and which she loved. She now had two very young children. I was two and my sister was a baby. The logistics of escape with two small children posed a challenge. Her brother Aleksandyr decided to go with her. Their papers had the same last name, and they could pass as a couple. Both were blonde and blue-eyed—my mother resembled their father and my uncle took after their mother.

My father was nowhere near the village. I understood that he was somewhere close to the Romanian border. I don't know how my parents managed to communicate with each other. Probably via the Resistance network. I know my father left separately. He already was a wanted man by the Allied forces, and by that time, he was also wanted by the Nazis. If they had travelled together, my parents would have been more likely to be recognised and arrested.

Time and again, my father's looks were his downfall. The jet-black hair and very blue eyes were not easily forgotten. He would not risk my mother's and his children's lives by coming with us. Besides, it was much easier to escape through uncharted routes alone.

In 2016, my sister and I met our relatives in Mostyska, the town where I was born. They made a fuss over us. My cousin took us to the local museum to impress upon us the fact that my father was a local hero. In the museum, there was a wall dedicated to the town's heroes. His picture was in the centre, surrounded by people who fought for Ukraine's independence.

There is also an oil painting, a portrait of our father that hangs in the town's community hall. The portrait was a surprise. I loved the portrait and cannot forgive myself that I didn't have the presence of mind to have it photographed.

We were presented with a book by the author called *Mostyska i Mostyshchyna*, a history of our region. It contained a few pages chronicling my father's work for the Organisation of Ukrainian Nationalists. His political activities made him a prisoner three times. He was arrested in 1934 and in 1938 by the Poles, and in 1943 by the Nazi Gestapo and sentenced to death. How he managed to escape was not described in the book.

This text is a challenge to read for someone not informed about that period. It is very detailed, listing many acronyms and different political groups. There is no glossary, as it is written for scholars researching the intricacies of that period.

My father talked very little about those days. He would actually joke about his prison record. He was proud of the fact that he was always able to organise a choir and lead his fellow prisoners in song. He loved to sing. His voice was powerful, and he had an amazing range. I have been reminded that he had perfect pitch. We sang very frequently as a family. My sister inherited my father's musical ear and has become a celebrated Ukrainian choir conductor in Canada.

My parents had agreed to meet before entering Austria. Their destination was a small town near the border. My mother told me they knew my father would have to be smuggled in, as he would never get through a German border crossing. My mother and uncle could easily pass as Germans; they fit the profile of Hitler's superior race. They were both fluent in German and could chat up the border guards in a casual and carefree way. They exchanged banter but didn't try to pretend they were Germans—that would not have been a smart thing to do. They were refugees escaping a war from a country occupied by the Allies at that time. But they were very good-looking refugees—my mother was beautiful, and my uncle had an appealing manner as well as a handsome face. The Nazis liked good-looking people sympathetic to their cause, even though, in this case, it was all pretence.

They were trying to get into Austria driving a wagon with a few belongings in the back. My father was hidden among their things. It doesn't seem to me to have been a very feasible plan. Perhaps the simplicity of it depended on my uncle's and mother's ability to charm the guards. But it worked! We were on our way to freedom.

There are three stories which I would like to retell. When I was a teenager I became aware of my father's active political past in the Resistance, I asked him if he had owned a gun at the time. He said he had, but he had never used it to shoot anyone. However, he had used it once, and he proceeded to tell me how.

He had escaped from prison with another young prisoner. The River Sian created part of the border between Ukraine and Poland. At night, the Russians scanned the river with searchlights. Anyone seen swimming across it was shot. The two runaways had to swim across the river to safety.

The young prisoner was terrified and refused to swim. My father said he had to pull his gun and threaten to shoot him. He said, "If you don't swim, I will shoot you. I will do it out of kindness, because if they catch you, they will do unspeakable things to you. Killing you is the least I can do for you." The boy entered the river, and they both swam across safely.

When they got to the other side, my father took great pleasure in belting out a few *alleluias* (Latin transcription of the Ukrainian), which echoed loudly throughout the region. I don't know what happened to the young man, but I hope he, too, found his way to a safe corner of the world.

My second story was told to me by my mother. In Canada, after my father's death, whenever I came to visit her, she wanted me to take her to the bank and go through her safety deposit box. It was always the same. A few treasures and a collection of Canada Savings Bonds. This was her security for her old age. The treasures were in a purple Crown Royal bag with a gold trim. A drawstring was pulled tight to hold all her cherished items safely. Every time we went to look through the safety deposit box, the treasures came out of the Crown Royal bag. These consisted mostly of a few gold trinkets and a few gold coins. She tried on her rings and other jewellery, which seemed to give her great pleasure. Once she took the bag, turned it upside down, and shook everything out. This was the first time I saw a platinum ring with small diamonds on it.

Knowing how much she liked things that sparkled, I wondered why she did not wear it. She sighed, "I have this ring because of someone else's misery. I cannot wear it ... But I should give it to you, because you were the child whose life would have ended if I had been caught hiding the local doctor, his wife, and their ten-year-old boy .... You take it and wear it. I cannot."

The family was Jewish. My grandfather, the priest, and the doctor were good friends. My mother knew they needed help when they arrived at the door. So she hid them and told no one. The Nazis suspected that the Jewish family would be helped by the local priest. They came twice and could not find them. A false wall in the cellar provided a good hiding place. Someone in the village, in order to save themselves, could have easily reported the doctor's and the priest's friendship, and the rest would be automatic. After the second time the Nazis came, the doctor's family felt they needed to move on. The wife insisted on giving my mother one of her rings. It's a lovely ring, now in my possession and noticed by everyone because of its shape and the unusual cut of the main small, elegant diamond. I can understand why my mother could not wear it—a painful memory, as she found out that, very soon after the family left, they were caught and shot.

There were other sad tales. One—my third story—I wish I had never heard. It was the plight of a young mother who had placed her baby on the straw in the back of a wagon. It was a soft place for the baby to sleep.

The young mother also thought it was a secure place, and that no harm could come to her child. The road was bumpy and the baby at some point rolled out of the wagon and onto the road. There was no going back, and she was inconsolable. I cannot imagine the horror of losing a child in such a tragic way.

These are the only stories that I remember. My great regret is that neither my father nor my mother would live long enough to know that we had reconnected with our family in Ukraine. But more on that later.

New Country, New Life

Only a railway separated our town in Austria from another country. We lived on the outskirts of town, in a big house in which we occupied one room. The house had a large yard, and at the very back of the yard was the railway line. If you crossed the railway tracks, then there you were, in another country. At least, that is what I was told.

In the summer of 1944, we left Ukraine and arrived in a small town situated close to the border of Austria. The border was unmarked and unguarded. The significance of that little detail was not relevant to me, but my parents had carefully chosen this place. It seemed safe—and just a few steps into a neutral country. Having survived the war, we had a very real concern that freedom could easily vanish.

Because of my young age, my wanderings were restricted. On one side of the house was the town's cemetery, which I enjoyed visiting and where I especially liked the flowers. On the other side of the house stood the police station. I spoke fluent German and liked to chat with the officers as they went in and out of the station. The chief of police was a very nice man and often engaged me in conversation. I considered him my friend, and I knew that I could rely on him if anything nasty should happen to me.

There were also other families we knew in that house. Each family occupied a room. Some were our friends and would join us for Sunday outings. This was something we all enjoyed and, on occasion, the outings included a train trip.

Very pleasant memories were the Sunday trips to the Alps, always with friends and always with a hamper of food. Every once in a while, looking out at the spectacular scenery, the adults would reminisce about leaving family, friends, and all that was wonderful behind, only to begin a new life in an unknown land. Tears would flow, but not for long. Such indulgences weren't helpful.

Occasionally, another family in the house would come along. Mrs. B could not accept that she and her family had to leave all that was dear. When she and her husband joined our outings, one could count on a scene. Despite the outbursts, my parents liked them, and understood the distress that tormented Mrs. B.

On one of these outings, after much drama regarding the exodus from the homeland, Mrs. B's husband lost his temper and lashed out with, "What do you want? You had a splendid outing, a grand lunch, good company, and a first-class view that few can enjoy .... Why the hell don't you just shut up?!"

What a revelation! My parents were not the only ones who raised their voices to each other. This was a comfort to me, because now I, too, could raise my voice in disapproval.

Before we left for Canada, my parents had bought a live rooster, which I considered my pet. I fed him and watered him and admired his beautiful feathers. He had a big cage, and occasionally, I would let him out, and then everyone in the house would run around trying to catch the poor thing. A few days before our departure, there was meat for lunch. Lunch was always the main meal. Since meat was very rare, I grew very suspicious. Where could it possibly come from? I rushed out to see if my rooster was still there. The rooster was gone. Into the outhouse I went, and there, at the bottom of the latrine, were feathers—many, many feathers. I tore into the police station and said to the chief, "Arrest my mother. She murdered my rooster!"

The chief pretended to take this accusation very seriously. He took my hand and walked me home, where he interrogated my mother and pretended to arrest her. Of course, she did not go to jail, as the kind police chief impressed upon me that if he arrested her, I would not see her for many days. I caved and said it was OK, she could stay—but not one bite would I take, nor would I be pushed into doing so. Many years later, when my mother told me this story, she was hugely amused by it all.

Is it true? I have no idea, but I did have a rooster that I remember very clearly, and I loved it. It was one splendid-looking rooster. Shortly after this murder, in 1948, we took a train to Italy.

In Genoa, Italy, we boarded the passenger ship *Gen. S. D. Sturgis* and sailed for Canada. This ship has a fascinating history. It carried troops and hundreds of refugees to various ports of the world. The crossing took eighteen days before we arrived in Halifax, the beginning of a whole new life was awaiting us. We docked on September 25, 1948.

* * *

It was good luck that brought us to this part of the world. There were options, as other countries were willing to take refugees from Eastern Europe. My father wasn't keen on the UK or the United States—he felt these countries were too imperialistic. Other countries like Brazil, New Zealand, and Australia were very far away. Europe was too unsettled after the war, too close to the tragedies and upheavals the war had created. And there was still hope that this would be a temporary arrangement, that they would be able to return to the land they loved, their family and friends. My parents applied for sponsorship, as did their friends. Most of our friends relocated ahead of us, and as soon as we had the papers, we, too, headed for Canada. My parents were pleased about our destination. After all, Canada was a country known to respect and value human rights. This was of great interest and very important to both of them.

Our family was one of many immigrant families that came in the late 1940s, early 1950s—first to Winnipeg, and later to Toronto, where we settled in the heart of the city, near Kensington Market. I have vague recollections of another, earlier life in a small Austrian town, a holding place for us before we undertook the long sea crossing to begin our life in a country called Canada.

Convincing us, the children, that this move to a new land was a good thing required some innovative thinking on our parents' part. My sister, Kvitka, and I were not at all enthused about embarking on this journey. My sister, being younger, was less of a problem than I was. I was not happy to leave, and rebelled by hiding in the cemetery on a daily basis, at the edge of the town. I do remember my pleasure in enjoying all the flowers in the cemetery, which I picked, though I knew this was not allowed. My parents had to give serious thought to my behaviour and to my resistance to the departure.

Also, I had started Kindergarten and was making new friends, whom I liked and did not wish to leave. And then, there was the fear of being inoculated against various diseases, a requirement for anyone hoping to enter Canada.

So, in order to encourage a more positive attitude toward the impending journey, my parents created songs and simple verses that would inspire us to accept the idea of leaving. These verses and songs were silly nonsense rhymes in Ukrainian, which we sang and recited with enthusiasm.

One song implied that Canada was such a wealthy place that all one needed was to survive the sea crossing, and the land of plenty would be awaiting. I was very fond of a little ditty which rhymes in Ukrainian, and which, roughly translated, goes ...

English	Ukrainian
I have a piece of bread	Маю кусень хліба
And a pound of jam	І фунт мармеляди
Keep well my friends	Бувайте здорові
I'm off to Canada	Їду до Канади

Other songs described a fairy tale land; where the streets were paved with gold and the chickens laid golden eggs. As preschoolers, we believed in all we recited and sang. However, my childhood dreams of a future homeland did not prepare me for our arrival at Pier 21 in Halifax.

I remember little of that crossing. The refugees slept on bunkbeds. The women and children slept on one side of the ship, and the men slept on the other side. If my memory serves me correctly, a mother and her children had to share a single bunk. My sister and mother occupied the lower bunk, while I slept in the upper bunk with a friend my mother met on the boat, Olha Malanchuk.

From the day my parents met Olha and Roman Malanchuk, a very close friendship was formed. They remained the very best of friends for the rest of their lives. There were other Ukrainian families on the boat, and there were also a number of children with whom we could play, though what games and how much freedom we had are not things I remember.

Most days, the crossing was pleasant, but we did suffer through one horrendous storm. We were all sent down to the sleeping area, and almost everyone was lying down as the ship rocked from side to side and pitched up and down. No one was steady on their feet, and there was an atmosphere of uncertainty and fear. The storm lasted through the night, and in the morning, the ocean was calm. Everyone was anxious to be up and out on the deck.

I am told that I was a particularly naughty child, and so was well known to the ship's crew. Such recognition did not always serve me well. One day, the crew was handing out oranges to all the children. I had never tasted anything so remarkable as that orange. I sneaked back into the line in hopes of obtaining another one. It was not to be. I was spotted and told unceremoniously that there would be no seconds, especially for naughty little girls like me. My first and only orange—the very best of pleasures for a very long time.

Then, one day, we were told that we would be docking in a short time. There was great excitement. My mother and I rushed to the side of the ship to see this magical land called Canada. As I peered through the boat's rails, I was devastated. Halifax stood before us, covered in a dreary, cold, damp mist. Nothing sparkled, nothing glittered, and there wasn't a speck of gold to be seen. I felt betrayed, and tugged at my mother's skirt, crying, "What have they done? They have brought us to the wrong country!"

Needless to say, this was not what I expected. Halifax loomed before us and shattered all my illusions of a good life in our new land. However, at the end of the ramp stood someone I knew, waving frantically. Someone I adored—Marusia, my mother's best friend, with whom I often stayed when she lived in Austria. In fact, in her eyes, I was perfect. I used to say to her, "My parents don't need me. They have my sister. Why don't you buy me?"

And here she was, waiting for us. I was delighted to see her! Unfortunately, a second disappointment was about to be revealed. A man stood beside Marusia. She introduced him as her fiancé. Instantly, I understood that I was no longer the most important person in her life.

We spent a day in Halifax preparing for our trip to Winnipeg. The next day, Marusia made sure we undertook the trip with plenty of food. She provided a hamper of cooked sausages and schnitzels—lots of good, garlicky food that would carry us through to Winnipeg.

On the train to Montreal was a small group of Jewish merchants whose parents had come from Eastern Europe. My father, who had a wonderful bass voice, had taught me many Ukrainian folk songs. For a young child, my repertoire was impressive.

The merchants heard me singing, and before I knew it, I was at the centre of them, belting out one Ukrainian folk song after another. They sang with me, smiling and wiping away the occasional tear. They placed a jar in the middle of the table and threw in a few coins for each song I sang. At the end of the trip, I had a jar full of silver coins—my first earnings on that remarkable trip from Halifax to Montreal.

Two days later, we arrived in Winnipeg and there, on the platform, were all the people who had left Austria ahead of us. There were flowers everywhere. I was hugged and kissed far too many times, and was pleased when the greetings were finally over. Then, of course, such a historic moment had to be documented. We arranged ourselves and the flowers on the platform for a group photo.

My mother, my sister, and I stroll around our town in Austria, waiting for our sponsorship papers to arrive.

Ready for Canada in our homemade winter outfits.

On the boat. My father, my mother, and Olha Malanchuk. My father is holding me, my mother is looking at my sister—but who is the child in the middle? I have no idea.

My grandfather's church in the village we left behind.

My maternal grandparents' elaborate graves, close to the church, up on the hill overlooking the village of Mysliatychi in Western Ukraine. I lived in this village, but I was born in Mostyska.

First Stop: Winnipeg

Winnipeg was a different world. Our new life in Canada began very humbly. My family shared the downstairs of a house with two other families. The downstairs flat had a kitchen, a living room, two bedrooms, and a bathroom. Each family had a room. We were a three-family unit. There were six adults and seven children. I remember afternoon rests as a compulsory way to ensure some private time for each family. We, the children, thought it a jolly arrangement. We loved it. Although life was fun for the children, I'm not sure how the adults coped in such cramped quarters. However, these were unusual times. Friends were needed; they helped you survive. Together, all of us rebuilt our lives, and our unusually steadfast, supportive friendships continued throughout our life in Canada.

All three families were sponsored by established and well-meaning Ukrainian community members in Winnipeg. How we ended up together in one apartment isn't clear to me. However, we were friends of the other two families from Austria and for the first year in Canada, this was the accommodation available to us.

Sponsorships were different in those times. There were jobs available, and in the 1950s, jobs secured food for the table and a roof over your heads. Not the case now, as jobs are not easy to find and assistance is critical at least in the beginning. We shared our resources—mostly food—so life had a communal living feel to it, in a relatively pleasant way. The house was safe and we were safe; the inconveniences seemed minor in comparison to our previous life.

Next door to our house stood a church with a huge yard. It was a great place to play, and it even had an ice rink in the winter. Of the seven children in the house, only one was much older and did not participate in our games. We got up in the morning and there was always someone ready to play. We tore around the neighbourhood, collecting others and organising games in the church yard.

That first winter, we found a dead sparrow. The bird was placed into a pocket and we hurried home to ask if we could put the little bird in the oven and warm it up, so that it could fly again. We were given an explanation of the meaning of death. It was incredible to us that the bird would never fly again. We, the children, had come through a war. However, death had no meaning for us, simply because we were so very young and our parents protected us from difficult images. So, here it was, a lesson on what death meant. It was a hard lesson. Subsequently, we had a funeral to organise, and that focused our attention for the rest of the day.

Our first Christmas in Canada arrived, and the families discussed what all of us would share for the Christmas Day meal. Christmas Eve is the most significant meal of the Christmas cycle. It is meatless, elaborate, and requires several days to prepare. Traditionally, we have twelve meatless dishes, which represent the twelve apostles. Adults fast most of the week before Christmas and no one eats anything during the day of Christmas Eve until the first star, symbolising the star of Bethlehem, is seen in the sky. Spotting the star was the children's job. It was an important job, as the meal could only begin after someone announced that a star had appeared.

Christmas Eve is referred to as *Sviata vecheria*, which, in English, translates into "Holy Supper." Before the meal begins, many families follow the old tradition of placing some straw on the table to represent the manger in which the baby Jesus lay. Over the straw, the family's best tablecloth is laid. The centrepiece is always a special braided egg bread (a symbol of prosperity) called a *kolach*. A round kolach represents eternity and in some homes, as many as three loaves are stacked one on top of each other. Usually, three candles are inserted and lit in the bread, symbolising the presence of the Trinity, the light in the world.

For rural folks who had livestock, their animals were fed before the family sat down to their own meal. There was a belief that on this Holy Night, the animals could talk, and no farmer cared to be spoken about poorly.

In our family home, it was our custom to invite a friend who lived alone, so that they had someone with whom to share the Holy Supper. Our other custom was to set a place for the family's dead in case their souls, *Dushi pomerlykh* ("souls of the dead"), wanted to join us for the meal.

We began our holy supper with the Lord's prayer, and then would sing one of the oldest Ukrainian Christmas carols, *Boh Predvichnyi* ("God Eternal"), which is traditionally sung on this evening. Then the host—*hospodar*—of the house offers a piece of blessed bread called *prosfora* with a little honey on it to each person. This bread symbolises Christ as the Bread of Life. The host greets each person with the saying "*Khrystos narodyvsia*" ("Christ is born"), and wishes each person good health, happiness, and prosperity. "Khrystos narodyvsia" is the greeting used throughout the Christmas season.

The dishes served on this holy night include *borshch* (beet soup), fish dishes, potato dumplings (*varenyky*), cabbage rolls, *uzvar* (a compote made with dried fruit), and the first dish of the evening, *kutia*, which is prominently displayed on the table. Kutia (a wheat dish) has the consistency of a watery porridge, and is made with produce collected from the garden: wheat, nuts, poppyseeds, and honey. Many cooks add raisins to the dish. The dish symbolises abundance, fertility, and prosperity. In pre-Christian times, the dish was prepared to appease one's deceased ancestors, but in Christian times, the dish represents the birth of Christ. Despite the symbolism, none of the children I knew were fond of this dish; however, we all ate at least a tablespoon to honour our heritage.

Kutia has been a dish ever since wheat was first cultivated three thousand years ago. There is a Christian legend about the origins of kutia. This legend states that when Joseph, Mary, and Baby Jesus were fleeing to Egypt, they passed a farmer sowing wheat. A miracle occurred: as soon as the wheat was sown, it was fully grown. The farmer was still in the field when the soldiers pursuing the Holy Family came along, inquiring if the farmer has seen the fugitives. He said he had seen them while sowing his wheat. As the wheat in the field was fully grown, the soldiers assumed it had been a while since the farmer had seen the Holy Family, so they gave up the chase. This is why kutia is served on Christmas Eve.

Christmas for us in the Slavic tradition does not include a gift-giving custom. Children receive gifts on December 19th, the feast of St. Nicholas in the Julian calendar. These are distributed by Saint Nicholas, a very serious and elegant saint. I have clear memories of our gifts from St. Nicholas. Every year, at the foot of our beds stood a package, and in it we found new underwear, a chocolate bar, an orange, and fifty cents. These were thrilling gifts, and for many years, we waited with great anticipation for December 19th to arrive. When I finally made some Canadian friends and saw the many presents under their Christmas tree, I was overwhelmed and confused. To this day, I think the custom of Christmas gift-giving is far too commercialised and puts many families at a disadvantage by pressuring them to buy more than they can afford.

The Christmas cycle ends on January 19th, on the Feast of Theophany, the baptism of Christ, popularly known as the Feast of Jordan. Again, there are traditional meals, but the traditions are more relaxed. We sing special songs called *shchedrivky*, which are quite jolly in nature. One well known *shchedrivka* in Canada is "The Carol of the Bells." Sung worldwide and translated into many languages, it is sung as a Christmas carol in English. It was written by Mykola Leontovych, who was murdered by a Russian agent in 1921. Leontovych's crime was writing music that inspired national pride.

Our first Christmas in Winnipeg was in 1949. My mother and Mrs. Max, also a member of our household, went to the market to buy the food for Christmas Day. Meat was now allowed, and so the two women came home with a big, dead white rabbit. Memories of tasty rabbit morsels inspired the purchase. However, there was a problem, as no one in the house knew how to skin the poor thing.

At some point, the house must have had a wood stove with a pipe that went through a hole in the wall above the door in the kitchen. And so, the white rabbit hung there for the day, until someone managed to skin it and cook it. I have no recollection of that meal and how they thought they could feed all thirteen of us with one rabbit. It seemed highly improbable. But there would have been other dishes characteristic of a traditional festive lunch.

I have no idea how we survived in terms of basic needs such as housing, food and other necessities. From time to time, opportunities cropped up that allowed us to manage and put food on the table.

Summer holidays posed a particular problem: what were the children to do while their parents went to work? My mother and a good friend decided that the new arrivals needed a daycare program with some structure. Many mothers took on work over the summer months, and their children needed a secure place to pass the day. So, a daycare was organised with a program that consisted of games, stories, singing, and dancing. All of it was fun, though we were especially keen on the dancing.

My mother was a trained preschool teacher who liked a certain structure to the day. Seeing that our lives were changing so dramatically and quickly, her daycare program gave us children some stability. You knew how the day would unfold, and most of us liked that a lot. Even the dancing had some choreography. Little dances were created for us, and everyone was included and important. The end of the dancing was characterised by a Ukrainian bow. The right hand on the heart, the left swung low and out with the palm of the hand facing the spectators. A traditional Ukrainian bow is an expression of thanks from the heart.

The children in the daycare. The first child on the far left is my sister,
with a white bow on her head. I am in the back, sitting next to my friend Vera.

The daycare children are enjoying a dance—well, some are, others aren't.

Lunchtime at the daycare. Sitting on my mother's knees is Larysa Hwozdulych, who grew up to work on some of my mother's causes. She was also the MC at my mother's funeral or Celebration of Life. My mother admired and respected her young friend.

Work or Adventure

That first summer in Winnipeg, my father and his friends needed work. No one spoke English, so it was hard to get. The women had fewer employment problems, as they could do domestic work or sew in the factories. But men like my father, who were well-read, had no handy skills. Someone in the Ukrainian community, who had lived in Canada longer and may have even been a Canadian by birth, took pity on them and devised an employment strategy.

Winnipeg is bombarded by mosquitoes all summer long. To solve this problem, a proposal was written to the Winnipeg City Council that encouraged the city council to consider a "death to mosquitoes" program. This proposal outlined how a team of people could be employed to spray the outskirts of the city with a toxic mixture and stop the infestation of mosquitoes on the gentle Winnipeg population.

And so, each morning, a truck pulled up and about a dozen or so men piled in and were driven to an area outside of town. The group of mosquito fighters were an unusual assortment of men. Most were professionals from Ukraine and some had been very active in Ukraine's underground fight for freedom. Not exactly a group of individuals one would imagine to be suited for this kind of work.

I would like to think they tried to eradicate the mosquitoes' breeding grounds, but I fear they quickly gave up and used the time in the country to entertain themselves. They read poetry, told stories, sang folk songs, held discussions, and shared their lunches.

Among the anti-mosquito brigade was an older man who had been traumatised by the war. He told stories—the most unbelievable stories—with great flair. That in itself amused the group.

Furthermore, he always featured himself in a most important role, often as a general. The men listened to him, humoured him with their attention, honoured his storytelling with applause, and referred to him as "General." He was affectionately called Yultsio. My father told me a favourite story of the general's. It had to do with the Second World War.

In this story, as the general, he was responsible for his troops. At one point during the war, he was faced with a huge problem. His army was surrounded and starving. Here, he would pause to impress upon his audience the gravity of the situation and then, in a solemn voice would state, "So, gentlemen, what could I do?" Another pause for effect. "I placed a call to my good friend Winston Churchill and told him of my difficult situation," (... a long pause ...) "and, what do you think happened?" Giving a dramatic sigh, he continued, "Why, gentlemen, the very next day, fifty thousand chickens arrived, and my men were fed!"

This was without a doubt a most improbable story—but not unique. Unfortunately, no one could forget the horrors of war. People seemed to cope by either reliving their trauma or creating fantasies—many rather humorous—to help build a resilience to the past, the sorrow and the loss that many endured.

And so, the small group of men passed the summer killing mosquitos for a little bit of time and, for the rest of the day, sharing their lunches and amusing themselves with stories and discussions. Humour was prominent and therapeutic, though there were also serious topics to be discussed. If I remember correctly, my father implied they drew up a rough talking outline and then took turns being responsible for leading the discussion.

Among this group was Myron Levytsky, already a distinguished Ukrainian artist, who became even more distinguished and well known during his life as a Canadian citizen. Levytsky was immensely popular and a whole lot of fun, but he did not take to the anti-mosquito battles and considered the whole exercise futile. The story goes that Levytsky simplified things right from the start. The minute they all got out to the outskirts, he emptied the canister of poisonous mixture under the first bush he saw and spent the rest of the day drawing and participating in the storytelling. The authorities caught on when they noticed that at every site, there would be one bush that immediately withered and died, whereas the mosquito population flourished. Once this observation was made, he was quickly fired.

Levytsky's drawings were impressive satirical caricatures. When his good friend Roman Malanchuk saw them, he wrote short, cryptic comments to go along with the drawings. Out of this partnership, the magazine *Komar* (*Mosquito*) was born. I remember the magazine, funny drawings and witty comments that delighted my parents. Unfortunately, Myron paid heavily for his satirical caricatures (often involving the clergy) and was refused commissions for painting the interiors of Ukrainian Greek Catholic churches for many years. Roman Malanchuk did not suffer the same fate, as he signed his texts with one of his twenty-seven pseudonyms.

* * *

Our second summer in Canada, my father was asked by the Ukrainian Canadian Congress to tour Western Canada and give speeches on various subjects of interest to the descendants of the pioneers who had arrived in Canada more than seventy years before us.

The very first wave of immigration came to Canada in the late nineteenth century, around 1880–81. Poverty drove the first immigrants to settle here. They concentrated mostly in the West, where they cleared and farmed the land and built a future for themselves and their families. These were hard and bitter years, and many suffered real hardships.

The second wave came after World War I. Immigration from Ukraine was more sporadic during the years between the two great wars. However, the Ukrainian population had increased in Canada. Families grew as life became a bit easier.

After World War II, the third wave of immigration from Ukraine to Canada consisted mostly of political refugees, writers, musicians, and artists, who had to flee in order to survive. With the arrival of this latest wave, there developed a great interest in the settled Canadian Ukrainian immigrants who had come before the war in reacquainting themselves with Ukrainian literature, history, traditions, and culture. By now, the previous immigrants/settlers were successful, and by the early 1950s, many had prospered.

By the time we arrived in Canada, most of the settlers in the West had established a way of life. There were town halls and churches, and people had a sense of living in a community. There were political and religious differences, but an interest in their common heritage created a keen audience for speakers who could present a lecture on a topic which appealed to Western Ukrainians.

My father had a reputation as an interesting and dynamic speaker. The committee asked him if he would consider touring the West and stopping in prairie towns to give lectures on whatever topics the people requested. He was delighted. He did not enjoy manual labour and was very poor at it.

Years later, we learned about his adventures on this job. He travelled from town to town by train. It was the best way for someone without a car to reach Ukrainian communities in the West. He would be met at the station and driven to a home where he was billeted. He enjoyed this, as it gave him an opportunity to hear stories about the first Ukrainian settlers in Canada's West. His hosts and the people he addressed in his lectures were descendants of the first Ukrainian pioneers. For him, this was an opportunity to learn firsthand about the experiences of Ukrainian settlers. It was of great interest to him.

He did have a problem. The train did not stop in every little town he was to visit. On one occasion, he was to visit a town where there was no train stop. Not knowing what to do or how to explain this, he pulled the emergency chord. The train stopped, and though the train conductor tried to question him, he received very little in return for an explanation, only a short statement: "No speak English." They let him off.

A year later he tried the same trick, but this time he had no luck. The conductor recognised him and indicated he should sit down and wait for the next stop to get off. He knew the game was up. He had not counted on being recognised. His lack of English, "No speak English," the handsome face, the jet-black hair and blue eyes—made it easy to remember him. The people who stood on the platform to greet him watched the train whip by and instantly realised the problem. Someone motored to the next town and picked him up. All was well.

The lecture tour proved to be a success, and he agreed to do another one. This time, he took me with him. I was trouble, too active and too busy for my own good. It wasn't a punishment—just a reversal of roles for my parents. At seven years of age, I toured Western Canada with my Dad. I loved the train, I loved staying in different houses with people who were always nice to me—and if they had children, what a huge bonus that was!

At home, we were always fed. Food was carefully dished out, and I have no recollection of being hungry. Food was treated with respect. You ate everything on your plate. It was not to be thrown out. To this day, I find it hard to chuck out a piece of bread. It gets chopped up and scattered in the parks for the birds.

I have one memory where I unintentionally broke the only egg left in the house. It was meant to complete the meal we were to have that evening. My mother looked at the broken egg and her face registered such disappointment that I thought I had committed a crime. Perhaps the broken egg recalled the years of nutritional deprivation my mother had endured during the exodus and the first few months in Canada. The egg would have made the meal tastier, but without the egg, it was mere sustenance, and not a pleasant dish. In that instant, her life seemed shattered, and like the mess on the floor, reality had to be dealt with, and she had to keep going. I remember this so clearly, because she looked defeated. She never raised her voice or said a word to reprimand me.

However, on the tour, everywhere my father and I went, we were treated extremely well. We were well fed. The abundance and variety of the food was exciting. Our visits created a party atmosphere, guests were invited, food was offered, conversation flowed. Although the food was a real feast, what I liked best was the ability to go out and play with the local children. Most of the time, we were billeted in villages and towns—and occasionally on a farm. Now, for a young child, the farm was heaven. The acres of space and the animals in the barn were all new experiences for me.

I went to all the lectures, sat in the front row, and listened attentively. I still remember a few things about the lectures—mostly the ones describing Ukraine's beloved writers Taras Shevchenko, Lesia Ukrainka, and Ivan Franko. All school-age children would have heard these names.

However, my father's lectures on Ukrainian history were lost on me. I slept through them. I knew people enjoyed his lectures. They surrounded him and bombarded him with questions, which he patiently answered. It was a popular tour, and the halls were packed with listeners. The receptions after the lecture were a treat. I had company—there were children and always a tasty something or other, not only for me but for any other children who came along with their parents.

We stopped in Vernon, BC, where my mother's brother, Aleksandyr Chomiak, was the parish priest. He lived in a small house surrounded by an orchard and quite a bit of land. He wanted me to stay with him for the days remaining in my father's tour. He thought it was a hardship for me to be dragged from house to house and to listen to my father's speeches. It wasn't, but this was even better.

He was my guardian when we fled from Ukraine in the summer of 1944. As mentioned before, my uncle and my mother escaped together, driving a horse and wagon with two very young children on board. My mother held my sister, at the time just a baby, and my uncle looked out for me as the wagon rolled along. My parents escaped separately—it was the only way they would make it to freedom.

As they were fleeing, my uncle told my mother that if the two of them survived their escape, he would become a priest, like his father. My mother laughed heartily, because my uncle loved to have a good time and she could not envision him as a priest. Once in Canada, he studied theology, married, and was ordained a priest. (Greek Catholic priests as well as Orthodox priests can choose to marry in the Eastern rite.)

He loved being a priest. I know he was much admired and respected. He was famous for his pleasant singing voice. It's important for a priest to sing certain services in tune, and wonderful for the congregation to be able to enjoy the music and have it well executed. His sermons were always short and to the point (something my mother always emphasised: "make it short, make it to the point"). He was very happy in his marriage and adored his family, getting much pleasure from his four children.

Many years later, when I was there, his youngest son, Andriiko, came running home from his first day in school. My uncle opened the door. "Andriiko, what are you doing here?" My very young cousin sobbed, "I don't like it! I don't like school at all!" My uncle put everything aside and sat Andriiko on his knee, and they had a chat. It took a long time to help six-year-old Andriiko agree to give school another try. If I remember correctly, my uncle negotiated a half-day school day for him, just so he could adjust to all the changes. He was a dear boy, very bright, and our family was devastated when cancer took him at twenty-four years of age.

Back to my visit to Vernon. I loved my uncle. He was kind and receptive to most of my ideas. He wanted me to have a good time. However, his housekeeper was not too keen on me. She was to take me home every night, as my uncle's house only had the one bedroom.

I quickly realised that my uncle's bed was wonderful. It was covered in old-fashioned duvets that were puffed up like clouds. After supper, I liked to climb into that comfortable bed and fall asleep. In truth, I was tired every night, since all day, I had climbed trees and had run around with other children in the area. I had a grand time.

Once I was under the duvet and asleep, my uncle did not have the heart to have me moved. He would say to the housekeeper, "Do leave the child here. She is asleep. Let's not wake her up. I can sleep on the couch." However, the housekeeper was not amused. She was onto me. She would have had me up and ready to leave with her. As far as she was concerned, the parish priest had enough on his plate and needed his rest in his own bed. He should not be sleeping on the couch while his niece occupied his bed as if she were a princess. She was nice to me, but I could tell she was not happy to have me around or to look after me.

Two weeks went by quickly, and my carefree summer holiday ended the day my father returned to take me home. We boarded the train and headed for Winnipeg.

Streetcars

The one exciting event that happened before we left Austria was the day the French troops came marching through on their way back to France. According to my mother, I darted out into the street and started to march beside the soldiers. I was sure of step and swung my arms, pretending to be one of them. I was full of bravado, as only a cocky preschooler can be. But to my horror, one of the soldiers turned toward me and pointed his gun at me. I ran for my mother and hid behind her. She tried to ease my fear by saying the solider was only teasing me. I didn't care if it was just for fun. I did not like it. But truthfully, the rest of the time, life in our town was very peaceful—very safe and very quiet.

The one other exciting event that thrilled us and the local folk was the international motorcycle race. The finishing line was close to our front door. Lots of friends and onlookers stood on the front steps to catch the sight of the winner coming down the road and stopping just past the finishing line. The street was packed with people who were eager to observe this very special event.

What a transition it was to finally land in Winnipeg—big and loud, with so much to see and do. A whole city for us to explore. My favourite thing to do was to ride the streetcar. Winnipeg had streetcars and perhaps even buses (but those, I don't remember). We used the streetcar, and it was so exciting to get on one and be whisked from stop to stop until you reached your destination. What was even more exciting was to be able to transfer to another streetcar and go in a different direction. For a young child who had just arrived from a very small rural area, riding a streetcar was as exciting as life could get.

The big city of Winnipeg grew smaller as we rode the streetcar and looked out the window at all the people, shops, and big buildings that lined the streets. There was nothing like this back in Austria. There had been no street-cars because there had been no need for them. I knew my way around my part of town, and we walked everywhere. It was a pleasant, peaceful town, a good place to wait for our more permanent future destination.

And so began my fascination with the streetcars that transported you from place to place. All kinds of people got on and off. Most impressively for me, there were women conductors who could drive the streetcars. My future career beckoned me.

The woman on our route wore an ever-so-smart uniform and a very perky hat that sat on her head perfectly. I wanted the hat and the uniform, but most of all, I wanted to be her when I grew up.

First of all, I decided that I would look very smart in a streetcar conduc-tor's uniform. The outfit and the conductor's seat at the head of the streetcar would allow me to announce the various stops along the route to the riders. At six years of age, I was really impressed with this job and the responsibility of getting people on and off at the right stop. My voice would have to be clear and loud enough for all to hear. I needed to practise this skill. And so, I dreamt that I would one day be the best female streetcar conductor in Winnipeg. My dreams about my future career were not to be, but at six, one should be allowed to pursue any dream. Reality is not a consideration.

My mother attended English school three times a week. One streetcar ride took her there. Most of the time, the same regular conductor was driving the car. We knew her from other rides, and so it happened that my sister and I made a solo trip to visit my mother in her English school.

Apparently, I was not happy to be left alone with the other two families in the house while my father was absorbed in his book. I managed to sneak my sister and myself out and onto the streetcar stop. "Where to?" asked the friendly streetcar lady conductor.

"To my mother's English school," I apparently had said, even though at this point in my life, English was not a language I had mastered. But I was six and I was confident.

We managed to get to the school. We knew where the class was and so we marched in as if we belonged. The English teacher was quite incredulous that the two of us, small and skinny, could find our way, on our own, to the night school.

It is quite unlikely that this actually took place, though my mother swears that it did. Questions remain. For example, how did we get out of the house? How did we pay for the ride? Could it be that no fares were charged to children under six? I'm not sure how plausible this story is, but I do know that people—strangers, in fact—were kind and helpful. However, I have to admit that my mother had no problem with exaggeration. It simply was a way of making a story more exciting. She justified a more dramatic version of events because they made us children feel more clever and capable.

What was undoubtedly true was that my mother's English class was very important to her. Her classmates were mostly Ukrainians who came to Canada at about the same time as we did. Some were our closest friends, and we saw them often. My mother loved her evening classes and would practise her English repertoire with her friends regularly. It was clear that the classes provided the group of learners with much fun and entertainment, because they laughed heartily when they talked about their night school. The teacher liked them and invited the class to her home for a Christmas party.

This was the group's first invite to a Canadian home. So, routes had to be discussed and planned. Streetcar numbers were posted on the wall in the classroom for all to peruse. The group decided on a meeting spot so that they would all arrive at the teacher's house together.

My mother's wardrobe was carefully scrutinised for the right attire. Mrs. B, who lived with us, was an expert seamstress and could carefully adjust whatever needed a tuck or two. My mother dyed her shoes to match her dress. She loved to do that, and continued this habit of matching shoes to the colour of her dresses for many years.

Of course, one could not go with empty hands, and so her fancy apple tart/pie—pliatsok, as it is called in Ukrainian—made its first debut in a Canadian home.

Years later, when we and most of the members of that English class lived in Toronto, there would be holidays and other festivities that the group of English students celebrated with great enthusiasm. Usually, after much food and drink, the singing would begin. The group had a repertoire that would carry them into the early morning. At the end of each party, before everyone went home, there would be a toast to the English teacher and to the three favourite songs that she had taught them. The evening came to a close with an emotional rendition of "My Bonnie Lies Over the Ocean," "It's a Long Way to Tipperary," and "Good Night Irene, Good Night." They were more than three simple songs. They were a symbol of their new life here in Canada, and of a place that promised peace and safety.

I have no idea what their English teacher thought of them, but she had a surprising influence on them and their thoughts about their new home. She taught them songs, and each song was immediately sung in harmony. Ukrainians love to sing songs that everyone knows as part of their common Ukrainian musical heritage, whatever the occasion. Some happy tunes, but mostly songs of sorrow: lost youth, lost loves, and most importantly, lost glory.

If I close my eyes and transport myself to that time, I can see myself sitting on the staircase, listening to their singing. They were well into their cups, but they sang all their songs with pleasure and in complex harmony.

Apple Pliatsok

A Ukrainian pliatsok is a popular dessert, a cross between a cake and a pie. My mother's pliatsok was deemed by her friends to be first-class. I have her recipe, and I have tried to recreate her pliatsok. Mine is good, but it is not nearly as good as my mother's. But it's worth a try, regardless. The list of ingredients is not in a logical order, but it's her list, and I have translated accordingly.

2 cups all-purpose flour
2 eggs
1 cup of sugar
1/3 lbs. of unsalted butter
2 tablespoons of Crisco
2 tablespoons of lemon peel (zest)
Juice from the lemon
A pinch of salt
1 tablespoon of baking powder
4 to 6 cups of peeled and sliced apples

There are no instructions in her write-up, but here are two ways of preparing this dessert.

Preheat the oven to 350°F.

Method A: Put it together as if you were making a pie crust. Put all the dry ingredients in one bowl and mix them. Cut in the butter as if you were making a pie crust. Add the eggs, lemon juice and zest, and mix till you have a soft dough. (I knead my dough gently). Put aside one third of the dough. Pat two thirds of the dough in to a buttered 9"x13" dish and poke a few holes into it.

Bake the dough for twenty minutes, until it is lightly browned.

Take the pan out and cool slightly. Add the apples and spread them over the dough. Take the rest of the dough and drop small pieces on top of the apples, almost as if you were making a crumble.

Bake for forty-five minutes or until a toothpick comes out clean.

Method B: I do not remember my mother pre-baking the bottom dough. She put the whole thing together and placed it in the oven. Once out of the oven, it had to cool. Then, she cut the pliatsok into two-inch squares. She dusted it with a little icing sugar and put the squares on a platter and served the sweets.

I like to add a few raspberries to give it some colour. Sometimes, I like to add chopped nuts. This gives the pliatsok some crunch.

This is a very forgiving recipe. It doesn't matter how you make it—I'm sure it will work out. I have tested both methods and received compliments from my friends. But then, they were my friends—who among them would say "this isn't worth eating"?

This basic pliatsok is often made with plums. Use all of the dough for the bottom crust. Cut the plums in half, remove their stones, and press the plums into the dough. Put the plums in tightly (cut side up) and bake till the dough turns a golden colour and the plums ooze out some juice. Allow to cool, cut the pliatsok into squares, and serve with a dollop of whipping cream on each. It's very, very good!

School

L ife in Winnipeg began to take on a routine. In an effort to maintain our traditions and culture, my mother and her friend Olha organised a daycare. As mentioned before, the program consisted of games, songs, and dancing. We all loved to dance. To my best recollection, this was only a summer program.

I started school in Winnipeg. Every morning, we marched to St. Nicholas School. This school was established in 1905, and its purpose was to teach Ukrainian immigrant children the English language. The school is now called Immaculate Heart of Mary. It was run by Ukrainian nuns, and during my time at the school, the nuns were rather stern-looking and imposing in their black habits. They were strict and at times harsh disciplinarians.

The language in the school was Ukrainian, and the only times we spoke English was when we read Dick and Jane and when we did math. Other than that, English was not used. My sister was too young for school, but somehow, she was allowed to stay with the nun who did the cooking. The cook was unique—a really kindhearted soul. The children liked her, and she occasionally hid us under the skirt of her black habit from whatever it was we didn't want to do.

Being late for school was not acceptable. There were severe consequences for arriving late to school. The awareness that one could be strapped for this caused a few of us to run to the back of the class, leap out the class window, and run for home. Jumping out the school window was another offence not considered acceptable by the nuns. Our class was on the first floor, and the windows were open in good weather. Parents sometimes intervened and promised to properly scold their children for poor behaviour. It seemed to me as if the whole world was afraid of the nuns.

One day, a group of us were strolling toward the school, and we decided that we would play the wedding game. Not really knowing what weddings were like, we got into the game with gusto. One by one, we married each other off quite a few times, and not always to the same partner. We created a ceremony that pleased us, but it took far more time than we realised. We arrived at school very late and explained that it was because we were busy getting married. That did not sit well with our teacher, a very strict nun, who used a wooden ruler to make us understand the seriousness of our actions. That whack, whack, whack sound as the ruler hit the palms of our hands certainly helped to eliminate any future thought of engaging ourselves in the silly wedding game. I do not remember ever playing it again. The threat of being disciplined and the memory of the ruler's stinging pain certainly gave one momentum to jump onto the window ledge, leap out fearlessly through an open window, and head for home. Quite exciting, actually.

On Fridays, the nuns supervised the playground and checked our sandwiches to make sure that no meat was tucked between the two pieces of bread. I often lost my sandwich because my mother was always in a hurry and would pack our lunches with what was available. Most Fridays, she would forget that meat was not allowed in school. But she always said that children should not fast because they needed to grow. She was right, as the Ukrainian Greek Catholic Church did not expect children, people over seventy years of age, pregnant women, and nursing mothers to fast. If only my mother had known the benefits of peanut butter, I wonder whether my Friday sandwiches would still have been hurled into the garbage.

Immigrants from Eastern Europe did not have peanut butter in their homelands, and so were suspicious of that particular sandwich spread. There was no one to inform the newcomers there were some new foods available to them that were nutritionally beneficial. We were introduced to peanut butter many years later.

That first fall in school, we had our pictures taken. Now, the nuns did have some flair and on occasion surprised us with some creative stage management. In September, a truck pulled into the schoolyard, and a few ponies came trotting out. A backdrop of a desert was arranged and a horse was placed in front of it. It was all so foreign to us. Most of us came to Canada by boat. We could identify with water and boats, but deserts and horses were exotic things we knew little about.

The horses seemed huge and unapproachable. We were very young children—some of us were tiny—and most of us were frightened. That was ignored as I was hoisted up on the horse. Although the horse looked peaceful, as soon as I landed in the saddle, it reared up. I was petrified. My photo is misleading because, though tears flowed, the wind blew my hair across my face, hiding my distress. I cried throughout the whole experience, which I remember vividly to this day.

My first two years in school were unpleasant. I hated school, I hated the nuns, and I paid very little attention to what was going on in class. Of course, one had to go. However, the social aspect of school was great. There were recesses and lunch breaks and lots of playtime after school, which kept us going without too much fuss.

Grade 1 picture. The nuns outdid themselves providing a background of an American desert. None of us knew anything about deserts and cacti. The horses looked mighty big and scared the life out of us. The nuns took no notice. This was a creative effort on their part. We would appreciate it eventually.

Moving to Toronto

After more than two years in Winnipeg, my mother was offered a teaching position in Toronto. It was a part-time job in a Ukrainian night school. She was a trained teacher, and this offer seemed to be a very good reason to move. Besides, it was something she really wanted to do, and Toronto held better opportunities for both my parents. And so, we left.

Eventually, we settled down and got on with the job of living in a big city. Toronto was a good place to be. We were surrounded by friends, in a community of newcomers who could relate, understand, and comfort each other.

Most of the families we knew lived in small quarters close to Bathurst Street, mainly between Bloor and Queen Street in downtown Toronto. We walked everywhere—to school, to Kensington Market, and to the various shops on College Street. It was an exciting place, and we thought we lived in the centre of the universe.

There were many different ethnic groups that had settled in our neighbourhood. Our public school's population was composed mainly of Italian, Portuguese, Jewish, Ukrainian, and Canadian children. There were probably others, but these were the groups I remember best.

We were befriended by another Ukrainian family, who helped us purchase a house. The house was a big brick structure on the corner of Bathurst and Ulster Street. Our two families shared the first floor. This family did us a huge favour, as it would have been impossible to purchase the house on our own.

We shared the kitchen—a big, spacious room that had a good-sized pantry that stored the dry food and necessities. There was also a tiny little room off the kitchen with a small single bed, which the adults enjoyed as a place to lounge, read, or nap. The little room also had a door to the garden, which we used to go in and out of constantly. Our family friends often opened the backyard gate and came into the house that way.

Our social life revolved around the kitchen. There was a gas stove, an icebox, a green table and six chairs, and a green velvet sofa, providing a comfortable seating arrangement. The green sofa was a popular place for everyone to perch on and chat. There were many long discussions—even some good-natured arguments among friends who came by for that very purpose.

Next to the kitchen was a double room separated by an arch, which was our bedroom and living room. In the bigger area, we had a pullout sofa and the dining room suite: a table made of cherrywood and five chairs, our first furniture purchase in Canada. In the smaller area stood a bed and a dresser and, for some strange reason, the record player, which we loved to listen to. We would join in with the music when it was familiar. Two slept on the bed and two slept on the pullout sofa.

The other family settled in the front room, and their daughter Lydia occupied a small room on the third floor. My sister and I loved Lydia. She was a high school student who wore neat, trendy clothes. She was very nice to us two annoying young children. To this day, whenever I am in Toronto attending a Ukrainian concert, I am always pleased to see her and exchange a few pleasantries and family updates.

My family enjoyed the kitchen and backyard more than the other family, who seemed to prefer the front room that was also their bedroom. Although our living quarters were very tight, we got along really well for two years.

After two years in Toronto, we were able to buy the house outright. This was possible because the second and third floor were rented out and the income helped with the mortgage. At first, we had mostly Ukrainian tenants, but later on, we became acquainted with Maritimers.

My parents were very sympathetic to these Maritimers. They were young, poor, and very, very homesick. They were trying to make a life for themselves in the big city. Quite a few rented a room in our house, but never for too long. They either ran out of money and left quietly in the night or—hopefully—found suitable employment and moved on to better quarters elsewhere.

I do remember a few of them. They used our phone to call home, since it was the only telephone in the house. They spoke Gaelic and often cried when they talked to family or friends. It was very sad. My mother would send food up to them. She related to their grief, as she wasn't that much older than most of them.

However, some of them were rather resourceful. Two fellows rented the large middle room on the second floor. They were quiet, and my parents were pleased with them. Then, one night, they had a party, which was still going full blast at midnight. My father pulled himself together and headed upstairs to tell them the noise had to stop. Since his English was very limited, I have no idea how he communicated with them. Somehow, he managed to make it clear that the other five fellows had to leave. Looking bewildered, the group of seven explained to my father that all of them lived there. Apparently, only two had keys to the front door and to their room. They worked odd hours, coming home at different times and would simply toss a stone to the second-floor window and wait for someone to throw down the key.

My father was impressed. He was highly amused that these young fellows had managed to outwit us for quite a few weeks. However, the gig was up, and away they went to another establishment—perhaps where the landlord lived elsewhere.

Vittorio and Luigi were two very pleasant, hardworking labourers from Italy. They did not speak English and my parents did not speak Italian, but they managed to communicate nevertheless. The two men cooked their meals downstairs in the basement, where there was a gas stove and there was a tiny fridge for the tenants to use.

Both Vittorio and Luigi liked their pasta. They also liked potatoes. They cooked everything the same way: in a really big pot of water that often had only two potatoes at the bottom. My mother tried to help them cook their food more efficiently, but they were set in their ways.

They stayed with us for several months and then moved on. I remember their friendly ways and the smell of parmigiano on their pasta. It was a foreign smell for us, and we could not believe that it would appeal to anyone. It was years later that I realised what I had missed. Parmigiano certainly makes a dish of pasta come to life.

Among our first tenants were Frieda and her six-year-old daughter. Frieda's husband was in jail, and she found herself in a difficult spot. The poor woman was juggling her resources any way she could in order to manage her life and her child. I am not sure what she did for a living, but every so often, she would end up in our kitchen for a cup of tea, having a chat with my mother—Freida spoke English, and my mother would practise her limited English. Once in a while, my mother and Freida would dance. I'm not sure why, but I know my mother was a very poor dancer, whereas Freida could gracefully twirl around the kitchen. Both laughed as they tried to keep in step with the music. I don't think my mother ever managed to dance with ease, a skill she would have loved to have had.

At that time, I didn't know much about Freida because I was young, but she struck me as a person who had a happy spirit and looked forward to better days. She didn't seem happy when her husband was released, but she left with him, and we never saw her or her little girl again.

I liked Freida and was sorry that she left. I liked the fact that she and my mother could have a good time despite the language barrier and the difference in their circumstances. Our life was improving, but I was not sure about hers.

* * *

In Toronto, my sister and I attended a public school, which was very different from our school in Winnipeg. There were no nuns who threatened you or intruded on your life. Though some teachers were demanding and at times unkind, I don't remember being afraid of them or of any corporal punishment they could hand out. The worst that could happen was that you would be asked to leave the class and sit outside the room or be sent down to the principal's office.

We attended King Edward Public School, which no longer exists. It was an old-fashioned building with lovely, wide wooden staircases and very spacious hallways. It was right on Bathurst Street, halfway down the block, on the opposite side of the street from our house.

Our first report cards from school stunned my parents. My sister's name had been Canadianized. Mine was fine, as I have a fairly basic, common name. My sister's name is Kvitka and her teacher asked her if the name had a meaning. My sister said her name meant a flower. So the teacher sent home a report card for Flower Zorych.

My father would not sign it. He took the report card and went to see the principal. In his very limited English, he tried to explain that his child was called Kvitka, no matter where she lived. He listed examples of names he was familiar with to make his point: She was Kvitka in France, not Fleur, Kvitka in Germany, not Blume, Kvitka in Spain, not Flora or Rosa. The principal quickly understood and the corrections were made immediately.

When the other co-owners of the house moved out, my mother started a small business in the front room which they had occupied. It was a cleaning business, and clothes were sent out and returned the following day. The business prospered, as there were many Ukrainians in the area who used the service, which helped the cleaning business get established. My mother could sew and was able to do simple alterations. This gave her a day job so she could stay home and take care of the house, the business, and her family.

I don't remember our elementary school principal's name, but he used to bring in his cleaning to my mother's shop. One day, he opened the door and a small puppy ran in. My sister and I were so excited! A great commotion erupted, with everyone trying to catch the little thing. The principal felt bad, because, of course, we could not keep it because it belonged to someone else. Tears flowed. Fortunately, the principal looked after the matter and calmed us children down.

After the fiasco, he was invited into the kitchen for a cup of tea and a slice of my mother's torte. My parents liked the man because he truly tried to understand and respect the diversity of his school. Subsequently, we were often sent to school on Monday mornings with a slice of torte for our principal.

As principal, he encouraged various ethnic groups to share their culture through displays of art, traditional artefacts, and music. Sometimes, different groups would offer the children a taste of a popular treat. If my memory serves correctly, the displays were held on the main floor and were open to the public in the evenings. They were a great boost to our community. My mother and her friends would meet to discuss how best to represent our traditions and culture. They put much effort into these displays, as they knew that this was one way to highlight what was important and dear to us. These displays were popular, as many of us attending the school were new immigrants to Canada. They helped build relationships and foster trust among the various groups in the neighbourhood.

King Edward School was not a large school. We knew almost all the students and the teachers. We loved the smell of the wooden interior and the large hallways. Later, in Grade Six, we would cross the schoolyard to enter the small building where the girls were taught how to cook and sew. The boys had a different program, but I am not sure what that was.

The school had two different alarm sounds, and we practised the response to each alarm on a regular basis. One was a fire drill, in which we loved to participate, because it was great fun. We had to slide down an enclosed, curved chute before landing in the playground. Not as much fun was the exercise we practised of how to protect ourselves should Canada become invaded by the Russians. This alarm indicated we had to dive under our desks to protect ourselves from potentially falling debris. The fifties were the age of the Cold War. We were not able to distinguish between a practice exercise and what might be real, so those alarms frightened all of us. Because of our parents' background, we were well indoctrinated in the politics of fear.

I have mentioned before that I don't remember being hungry. However, we arrived in Canada with distended stomachs, as the food we had eaten in the years before lacked variety and was, unfortunately, not very nutritious. My mother said, that only once in Europe, the Red Cross helped out by distributing milk. From the time we left our homeland to the time we arrived in Canada, healthy food was a luxury not available to us. After a few years in Canada, however, my parents built up some credit and everything started to improve.

At King Edward School, there was a school nurse and a doctor who visited once a week. When the doctor first saw us, he was very concerned because we looked malnourished (and probably were). Both my sister and I were sent to High Park for summer school. I don't think my parents knew or understood that this was a school for poorly nourished children. They were encouraged to consider how the summer school program was designed to give children extra academic help in English and math. My parents were keen for us to do well in school, and to them, anything that would focus on helping children develop their language and math skills had to be a good thing. It really was a very carefully laid out remedial program for those of us struggling on any level.

In Winnipeg, we had hardly spoken any English, since we had lived in a totally Ukrainian environment. So, off to summer school we went. It was great for us, because they provided snacks and a healthy lunch, as well as lots of outdoor play. We even learned how to play baseball. That was worth a lot, believe me! Our English was also improving.

* * *

Somehow, while still in elementary school, I saved six dollars. It took a long time. It had to come from my Friday treat money—I was given twenty-five cents a week to buy a milkshake at the restaurant around the corner from the school. I also had a job. Every Friday night, I was employed by the local synagogue on Markham Street to shut off the lights in their place of worship. The synagogue was just around the corner and the light switch was easily accessible, so this job was not a hardship at all.

I think I might have gotten this simple job because of my friendship with Helen. Helen's family arrived in Toronto a few months after us. They were a Jewish family, originally from Poland, and the family spoke Polish at home. They had no English at the time.

Helen was enrolled at my school and ended up in my Grade 3 class. The teacher quickly realised that Helen and I could communicate. Polish and Ukrainian are Slavic languages with many words in common but different alphabets. Helen and I could chat as long as the language we spoke to each other was fairly simple. I could help her and interpret almost everything the teacher wanted her to know. Helen was very smart, and my interpretation skills were not needed for long.

We became good friends and often played together, either at her house or mine. The family did not stay in our neighbourhood for long, and moved to the north of the city, where there was a large Jewish community. I was invited to visit, and went a few times, but eventually, we lost touch with each other.

The six dollars took almost two years to save. I splurged all of it on a pair of hideous blue pedal pushers, which were the rage in those days. My sophisticated, art-loving mother shuddered when she saw me in the pedal pushers, but I thought they were simply splendid.

Living on Bathurst Street was busy and exciting. There were many young families with children, and we quickly made friends, roaming the area in our neighbourhood together. Crossing Bathurst Street was out of bounds, as it was a wide, busy street with streetcars going north and south on it. The neighbourhood children with whom we played came from different ethnic backgrounds.

I didn't like school, because children who were new to Canada were ridiculed and called names. It was not uncommon for me to be told, "You cannot play with us, you dirty little DP." I did not understand the reference, and I'm sure the children calling out the insults knew it was an unkind name, but they didn't know that the term "DP" meant a displaced person. So I did not take offence. Nevertheless, it was quite true that one glance at my outfits indicated I was rarely clean.

My mother put a clean dress on me every Monday, and it had to be worn and kept clean all week. It rarely was. Underwear was changed every day, but no one saw the clean white undies I wore under my dresses.

Besides the cleaning business, my mother worked at a variety of Ukrainian community-based jobs, and really did not have the time or energy to ensure that there were no spots on my clothes. And sadly, I did not care. Once a spot appeared, the pressure to stay spotless evaporated.

Despite the name-calling, I do have some very pleasant memories of my time at King Edward School. Every year, a small and roundish man came to our school and chose two children—one from Grade 5 and one from Grade 6—to sing in his Toronto Children's School Choir. As a child, I had a pleasant voice, and was picked to sing at Massey Hall. There were five hundred of us from various schools in Toronto chosen to sing in the choir.

Our choir outfits were simple. A white dress, white socks and black shoes for the girls; and the boys were to show up in a white shirt, black tie, black pants, socks, and black shoes. My mother designed and made a white dress for me that had a little crinoline (all the rage in those days), which made me feel very smart and professional on that stage.

It was a huge event and such a thrill to participate in this choir. There were responsibilities. For example, you had to get yourself to Massey Hall for rehearsals. However, you were allowed to leave school right after lunch to get there on time. I loved the whole experience, the rehearsals, the responsibility of learning all the songs in the music booklet, and the grand performance at the end. I remember belting out "O Sole Mio" and the other songs, and I can still remember all the words to the song which ended the concert:

My Country is My Cathedral

My country is my cathedral
The northern sky its dome
They all call it Canada
But I call it home

The mountains, the lakes and valleys
Are friends that I have known
They all call it Canada
But I call it home

From the Atlantic to the Pacific
From the Pole to the USA
We're one united brotherhood
And united we will stay

The people across the border
And far across the foam
They all call it Canada
But I call it home[1]

It was such a thrill to be part of a group of five hundred ten and eleven-year-old children with a full orchestra accompanying us as we sang our little hearts out. The audience filled the auditorium and stood up to honour the patriotic song—and we had the power to inspire their standing ovation. As it was the last song of the program, the concert ended with thunderous applause and cheers from the audience. It was wonderful.

In those days, Massey Hall seemed incredibly large, ornate, and majestic. As a child, it seemed to me that only very special people were allowed to perform or go there. Eventually we, as a family, did attend a few concerts at Massey Hall. It was always a thrill, a very special occasion for us. We dressed up in our finest clothes and headed to the performance. And this time, there

---

1   Fritz Grundland, *This Is Canada: Songbook with Sheet Music for Voice and Piano with Chords* (Toronto: Gordon V. Thompson, 1967).

I was, up on the Massey Hall stage, one of five hundred children, singing as one voice in this enormous and lavish venue. That really was a phenomenal experience!

Bathurst Street brings back the memories of my schooldays—days spent in elementary school and high school. Harbord Collegiate was my old high school, where I formed a few friendships that have lasted to this day. I did not enjoy elementary school, but I loved my days in high school.

First of all, there were so many students—far more than in elementary school. Lots of Ukrainians to chat with—but also, students from different ethnic groups were interested in being friends with us, in part because our English was much improved by then and we could communicate with others.

In high school, I took a music class. My earlier experience of learning to play the piano was not successful. My music teacher indicated I should give up piano lessons and save my parents their money.

In school, I tried the violin, but that was a hateful experience. Those high squeaky notes were too much to bear, so I thought a cello would suit me better. I liked the cello, with its velvet sound and no high, squeaky notes. My mother was not so keen to have a friend and I practising our instruments in our basement. She offered us twenty-five cents to play our cellos somewhere else. Despite her lack of encouragement, I managed to get a place in the school orchestra. I was not a particular asset to the orchestra, as I was so nervous about playing for an audience that I faked it by moving the wand close to, but not over, the strings.

Night concerts and other social events were part of the school's community outreach program. My parents came to the school concerts with friends from our Ukrainian community, and they seemed to enjoy these evenings.

As I sat in the orchestra, pretending to play the cello, I knew where and when my father was in the audience. He had a powerful bass voice, and his friend Mr. Max (who had two children and a nephew attending Harbord Collegiate) had a strong tenor voice. You could hear them singing "God Save the Queen" because they could out-sing everyone. Of course, they sang the words in Ukrainian.

I just wanted to disappear. As a teenager, I did not wish to be noticed, and I sure didn't want anyone to know that the bass voice singing in a foreign language belonged to my father.

Sunday Sermon

On Sunday mornings, we dressed up in our best outfits for church. I didn't like church very much. The sermons seemed to be endless. The parish priest was old and mumbled most of the time. Attending church on Sunday mornings just seemed something one simply had to do. However, from time to time, the old parish priest did have a way of focusing the parishioners' attention. He was of another generation, having arrived in Canada before the First World War. He spoke Ukrainian occasionally interspersed with English words. Immigrants who had lived in Canada much longer had no trouble understanding him.

One of the first sermons that we heard described Lazarus's remarkable recovery from a severe illness, and the elderly priest's telling of it was inspiring to all.

The old parish priest, having finished describing Lazarus's illness, paused, looked out at his congregation, and solemnly said, "And where do you think Lazarus went after his remarkable recovery?" (A pause.) "Do you think he went to a bar to celebrate his newfound health?" (A pause.) "Or do you think that perhaps he went to a dance hall?" (Another pause.) "Or perhaps he went on a picnic?" Then, there was a very long pause as we waited for him to enlighten us on where exactly Lazarus actually went. Oh, the suspense of it all!

The old priest looked at the congregation and declared. "No, no, my friends, Lazarus did not go to a bar, or a dance hall, or on a picnic to celebrate his newfound health. No, my friends, he went to God's house where he fell on his knees and gave thanks to the Lord."

This sermon was a trifle confusing to understand, not because of its depth but because what in Heaven's name did the words "bar," "dance hall," and "picnic" mean? We, the newcomers to Canada, were bewildered. Half the congregation had no idea what those words meant. Understanding came when more enlightened folks were able to explain not only the words but also the analogy.

It must have been a very unique experience for my mother, the daughter of the village priest. My grandfather was described as a serious scholar of religious teachings. Most religious traditions and customs were and still are tightly intertwined with Ukrainian values and practices. I was told that he knew Hebrew, as many priests did in those times, and also spoke three other languages. That was not unusual for someone living in Europe, however—most educated Europeans spoke at least two if not three or four languages.

I can't help but wonder how my mother accepted this unique interpretation of the Lazarus story. How bizarre this service must have sounded to her, but she was willing to accept it as a learning experience and an example of how different things could be in a new country. My mother also admired the old priest's ability to relate to both the regular congregation members and the new arrivals by using references that piqued everyone's interests. New words and new experiences awaited us as we adapted to our life in Canada.

A few weeks later, the priest announced a church picnic. He actually used the word "picnic." Here was our opportunity to experience this elusive event. We piled onto a bus with our lunches and headed out of the city. It was a good day. We had a lot of fun, and picnics became a tradition for our family and our friends. We felt we had adopted a Canadian custom and given it an ethnic twist—especially where the food was concerned.

We picnicked most Sundays with at least three or four other families. When we first began this tradition, no one had a car; a streetcar took us out to a farm on the outskirts of Toronto. The farm was the property of a Ukrainian community centre, and was popular because there were lovely trees and a lively brook that flowed through the property. Rain or shine, swimming was always part of the agenda. I think that in most cultures there are picnics, perhaps with some variations as to the way we enjoy them. Picnics provide a relaxed way for people to mingle and get to know each other. Although they might have been different in Canada, they weren't a completely foreign experience.

Things were beginning to look up. Our lives were busy, our leisure time was good fun, and on numerous weekends, we enjoyed cultural activities like concerts and plays, which were well attended. They gave us a chance to keep in touch with friends who did not live in the neighbourhood. Life was good.

The church has always been a strong factor in our community. I do not know of anyone in the Ukrainian community who did not attend church. Families went whether or not they were religious. My father could sing a liturgy without any sheet music. He was particularly interested in our church music. In Ukraine, he always sang or directed the church choir. I am not a religious person, but I love the music of our church services. It is melodic and often haunting. In Toronto, I go to church to listen to the music. It is a spiritual event for me.

In my teens, I was allowed to have a small glass of wine on Sundays. The jug of sacramental wine was a gift from the bishop. I found this wine to be very sweet, and I was not sure whether I liked it or not. However, it did teach me not to indulge, as a little went a long way.

Ukrainian School

The job offer my mother had in Toronto was regarded by my parents as a worthwhile proposition, and our family settled down in the heart of the city. Classes were held three times a week, from five to seven in the evening. The private, non-profit school was located on College Street, near Spadina, one block east of Kensington Market.

I do remember some of the teachers from the school, as they were part of our social life. Olha Malanchuk, a trained teacher, taught Grades 1 and 2, my mother taught Grades 3 and 4, and Tonia Horokhovych taught Grades 5 and 6. Olha Malanchuk was a very close family friend. After all, I shared a bunk with her on the ship upon which we crossed the Atlantic Ocean. Tonya Horokhovych was involved in the Ukrainian Scouts with my mother, and they became very good friends. These were creative and talented women who recognised that besides an academic focus, a school could provide the community with a sense of belonging, a sense of pride and entertainment, something that nurtured the community and validated them as worthwhile citizens.

Our communities enjoyed concerts or theatrical productions. There were quite a few community halls, which provided a venue for such activities. The staff at the Ukrainian school decided that the children in the school would benefit from putting on a three-act play—a musical, no less. This was not a shabby production. Everyone was involved: children, parents, school staff, and community volunteers. Mr. Levytsky designed the costumes and Olha Malanchuk choreographed the dances. My mother directed and coached us to perfect our parts—we children were the actors.

A special effort was made to include all the children who were interested in performing in the play. Those too young to perform were flowers that danced as the wind blew, and still others were part of the scenery. No one stood still for very long—especially not the young ones. Everything moved to the music.

A few weeks later, the play opened to a full house. The performances were well attended, as they were always social occasions, excuses to see and mingle with others in the neighbourhood. Besides, a production performed by children was always fun to watch.

The play was about a little bird that wanted a more exotic look. But where to obtain this exotic look? The little bird decides to fly to Africa in search of fancy feathers and a more stylish lifestyle. Roughly, the title translates to "In Foreign Plumage."

Of course, the moral of the story is to be happy with who you are and grateful to live among family and friends who care for you and love you. This difficult lesson is discovered by the little bird as it sits in the tall grassland of Africa. It is sad and lonely. There is no family, nor any friends, to cheer the little bird up. A simple little lesson done in verse, song, and dance. Needless to say, this was my first stage performance. As a child, I not only had a pleasant voice but the confidence to strut about the stage in my role as the African night. A silver moon was perched on my head. A black lace veil flowed from it and draped itself onto the floor. Silver stars decorated the veil. I held a spindle in my hand and spun out the night. I sang the night song, in which I cover the daylight with darkness. I thought I was splendid in my beautiful long, black gown, the moon on my head and my veil full of sparkling stars, as I kept vigil over Africa.

And lo and behold, I, as the night, find the little bird weeping in the grass, homesick and lonely. The night lady misses nothing, and she encourages the little bird to tell her what it is doing so far away from home. The unhappy little bird spills out its sorrow. "Go back home," says the night lady, but the little bird needs more encouragement to do so. And so, the play continues.

The play was performed a few times in Toronto, and the costumes were elaborate and beautifully designed. Eventually, I lost my role to a better and stronger voice. It was someone else's turn to shine.

There was a perk for those of us who lived near the school. After the rehearsals for various performances were over, we headed for Kensington Market, located one block away from the school. The market stalls presented us with a wonderful venue for a game of hide-and-seek. Instead of heading straight home after school, we made a detour by the market. Boundaries were laid out and the game of hide-and-seek began.

We tolerated school because of the extra-curricular activities we indulged in later in the day.

The cast from the play In Foreign Plumage.

The youngest students are the dancers. They are the poppies that dance as the wind blows. Olha Malanchuk choreographed the dances and taught the children how to move gracefully. Her daughter, the youngest poppy, is the second from the right, in the front row. The petals were red and the collars and undies were green. Notice the poppies on their heads.

The audience watching the production.

Here I am as the night, who spins out the darkness.

* * *

Later on, during high school years, most of my friends and I had to attend Ukrainian high school, every Saturday morning from 9 a.m. to 1 p.m. The school was on the very top floor of the church. As I climbed the steps that took me past the church balcony, I truly felt I was making my way up to Heaven. It was a feat to get up there. There, under the church's roof, were three classrooms. Besides the physical effort needed to make it to school, there was the mental agony of trying to get the assignments done on time.

This was hard work. Many a Friday night, while my Canadian friends had fun entertaining themselves, I worked on the assignments due the next morning.

We were required to memorise lengthy pieces of verse written by Ukraine's most celebrated poets. I liked the dramatic ones, the patriotic ones, and the simple, lyrical ones. Poetry came easily for me. When rehearsing the material, I would pretend I was doing a poetry reading that had the audience mesmerised, sitting on the edge of their seats. Ukrainians like poetry, and most of our concerts paid tribute to the music and poetic words of our famous writers, such as Taras Shevchenko, Lesia Ukrainka, and Ivan Franko. Our Ukrainian high school principal was not a woman to listen to any excuses. She was short and solid, with a look that said don't mess with me. She taught us literature and knew her stuff, but she rarely inspired students to love what they had to read.

A few years after I graduated from the Ukrainian high school, the church built a new building and moved the Saturday morning classes there. This was a bigger building with bright rooms. My mother became the principal. I was studying at Ottawa University then, but I can only imagine her effort and dedication to doing the job well. By this time, I was very pleased to be finished with school on Saturday. It was a memory of a hateful time for most of us who had to attend. At least the students were no longer expected to learn pages of poetry. My mother chose shorter works for students to memorise.

My mother's high school students—my friends now—confided that she, too, was feared by many of the pupils. No one came to class without doing their homework. You did your work. And if, by chance, you had to face a dressing-down by her, she would scold you, but also make sure to give you a little compliment as you marched out the door.

My friend Olenka told me that after one such scolding, my mother opened the door for her to exit and, as she passed through, patted her on the head and said, "Nice hair." I never had my mother as a school principal, since by this time, I was enjoying my freedom and university courses. This story of her working hard to try to balance discipline with kindness surprised me as I knew how demanding she could be.

When she passed away, people came to offer their sympathy, express their condolences, and acknowledge our loss. Traditionally, we have a short service the day before the funeral and people make time to chat with the family. It's different from the wakes held in the Maritimes. During the event, I met quite a few of her previous students. Some shared their experiences of their time in the classroom with my mother. I'm sorry I didn't jot the stories down, but the one thing that was clear was the respect the past students had for her, despite, and perhaps because of her strict disposition and her little compliments, which seem to touch them and amuse them.

Students were required to take six subjects: literature, history, religion, architecture, creative arts, and geography. At the end of our high school years, there were oral exams. These were conducted by a panel of our teachers, and each teacher would ask a series of questions pertaining to their subject. You had to pass all the subjects in order to graduate and attend the graduation dance.

This dance was attended by all the graduates and their families. It was quite the production. I had a dress designed by Mr. Levytsky and made by Mrs. B. Mrs. B was a skilled tailor, who could make anything you wanted. We'd show her a picture, and it was never a problem for her to reproduce the outfit. Every once in a while, she would mumble, "This dress is too short" or, "This neckline is too low." She'd say, "Does your mother know what you are asking me to do? I don't want any trouble. Oh dear, I need to have a cup of tea." Tea always indicated she did not approve of the design.

On the other hand, Mr. Levytsky was great fun and a daring designer. He was happy to create original designs for our special occasions. I loved my graduation dress. It was made of white organza, as all the girls wore white dresses.

My dress had a square neckline and a full skirt with a puffy crinoline underneath. The skirt was covered with small, plump bows that gave the dress a rich and elegant look. Mr. Levytsky had done a grand job, and I received many compliments.

The graduation celebration began with a festive dinner, followed by a dance with a live band. Of course, there were a few speeches during the meal. The graduates were recognised and applauded. Pictures were taken, and finally, the music started and the dance began.

My father always danced with me at least once—sometimes twice—and as he was such a good dancer, he would instruct me as he twirled me around, saying, "Now your right foot, now your left; hold your head up, and now we'll spin around." Waltzes, I could manage well, but tangos were tricky, and I was glad to see him coming to guide me while I stumbled through a difficult number. After the dance, he would escort me to the table, where I sat with my friends. When it really mattered (in front of my friends), his manners were impeccable.

Luxuries

Our house on the corner of Bathurst and Ulster Street was very large. The brick structure came with a garage at the back of the yard, and all of it was considered rather grand because of its size.

Thanks to its size, my parents were able to rent out many rooms—mostly to friends in the beginning. Renting to friends provided a social atmosphere in the house while giving them time to find their own, more appropriate lodgings.

But what really caught everyone's attention was our car, the dark green Desoto. To this day, how my father managed to acquire a car is a mystery because of his modest income. My guess is that he worked another job instead of attending English classes, as owning a car seemed far more attractive to him than spending time at night school. After all, he could and did derive great pleasure from his car, whereas being in a room full of people he could not communicate with three evenings a week seemed a waste of time.

On the other hand, the car, the beloved Desoto, created a great deal of excitement. Cars were owned by very few people in our community. Almost no one owned a smart, dark green Desoto with its own garage in which it was carefully and lovingly parked at night.

The car was not used on a daily basis. It was only driven on special occasions, such as to church on Sunday or to concerts. On Sundays, our doorbell would ring multiple times, and each time, a smiling, eager face would look at my father and request a drive to church. There were many Sundays my father drove to church two or three times, as he could never refuse a child the pleasure of arriving at church in a car.

Though a car was a luxury few could afford, life as immigrants was not easy. As a community, we kept our spirits up by entertaining each other in a variety of ways. Oh yes, there were concerts, poetry readings, and dances, but for the children, the best were the meals we shared with our closest family friends. These were long, drawn-out affairs, often with enough children in attendance that there was never a problem in organising active and noisy games.

One morning, a formal-looking, hand-addressed envelope arrived by mail. It was an invitation. We were very excited and there was great speculation as to what the occasion could possibly be. It was an invitation to a dinner to celebrate the acquisition of an electric refrigerator by our friends, the Malanchuks.

My sister and I certainly knew what an electric refrigerator looked like. We knew with certainty that an electric refrigerator was so much grander than the icebox in our kitchen. We had often pressed our noses against the windows of the Rochester Appliance Store on College Street and marvelled at the splendid white refrigerators that stood in a straight line behind the display window. Finally, at last, we knew someone who owned the genuine thing.

The invitation came from Roman and Olha Malanchuk, my parents' closest friends. They lived on Markham Street, not too far from us, and would often drop by for tea and conversation. Mr. Malanchuk enjoyed the company of good friends and would often sit on our kitchen sofa and tell wonderful stories. The kitchen sofa was the venue for our family's social gatherings. We did not have a proper living room, but our kitchen was large and could accommodate the all-important green velvet sofa and all our guests. Stories were exchanged, along with laughter, sympathy, and at times, tears. Telling stories was a way of life in our community. They amused us, nourished our souls, and validated us as a people.

So here it was: a printed invitation delivered by mail. It certainly was a worthy conversation piece. The printed message promised a lavish dinner with an unusual twist. This event offered a program that showcased the talents of those present.

How did Mr. Malanchuk manage to present us with such a formal, printed invitation? Well, he was a writer and an editor in the Ukrainian language, well known for his literary and editing skills. His first job in Toronto was as an editor of a Ukrainian newspaper. This gave him access to a printing press, so it was not difficult for him to produce these printed treasures. After my mother's death decades later, as I sorted out her papers, I found a copy of the program for that evening. It was such a stroke of luck to find that small, printed invitation, it was better than winning a lottery!

What Mr. Malanchuk decided would truly make this refrigerator purchase a celebration and a memorable occasion was to assign speeches to the adults who would be sitting around the table. He knew his friends very well, and each speaker had no problem tackling the subject and entertaining all of us royally. I am very certain that Olha played a significant part in creating this event.

But first, a look at the translated invitation (see below). Maria Malanchuk translated it for me. Like her father, use of proper language is imperative to her.

Now, you need to be introduced to the speakers. The Malanchuks' guests were Mr. Karmanin (Mr. Malanchuk's childhood friend) and his wife Olha Kovbel; Mr. Levytsky (also Mr. Malanchuk's childhood friend); my parents, Bohdan and Yaroslava Zorych (close friends of the Malanchuks); and three children: Maria, my sister, Kvitka, and myself. All of the adult guests except for Ms. Kovbel were Ukrainian political refugees who had arrived in Canada before 1950. Ms. Kovbel was not a recent immigrant to Canada. As far as I know, she had been born in Canada. She fascinated us because she sported her hair in a smart bob and wore beautiful, store-bought clothes and lots of jewellery. She possessed a regal bearing and always smiled at everyone. She did speak Ukrainian, but with a slight Canadian accent.

The speeches were great fun, and the topics which appear on the invitation (see below) spoke for themselves. However, the highlight of the evening was five-year-old Maria, who stood on the piano stool and recited a poem written by her father entitled "My Own Dear Refrigerator."

It was a grand party, a wonderful feast, and one of my most treasured memories of a time when we had little but knew how to have fun.

Though the fabulous event provided us opportunities to tell of how an electric refrigerator was now standing elegantly in the Malanchuks' kitchen, my sister and I knew our beloved Desoto was no longer the most exotic thing in our community. The electric refrigerator was a luxury that only one family we knew owned and used on a daily basis. We piled into the car to go home and I secretly whispered, "I'm so sorry. You've been upstaged. But it's OK—in our family, you're still the best thing we have!"

Olha, Roman, and Maria Malanchuk
have the honour of inviting
YOUR EXCELLENCY
to participate in a GRANDIOSE FAMILY CELEBRATION
which will take place on Monday, October 12th, 1953 at 6 p.m. in the
salon of their residence (191 Markham St.) on the occasion of the
purchase of their very own
R E F R I G E R A T O R
Brand: McClary, Deluxe 1953 model, 7.6 cubic feet, comprising a
special "Butter Conditioner" with separate temperature control
Price: ... (?) – a surprise for the guests!

PROGRAM
1. The unveiling of the refrigerator
2. A solemn minute of silence
3. The festive announcement of the refrigerator's price
4. An even more solemn minute of silence
5. Applause
6. Congratulations
7. Salutations
8. Ovations
9. A cycle of academic presentations:
a) The Refrigerator and the Increase of the Consumption of Beer: The
    Main Objective of New Canadians – the Hon. Yu. Karmanin
b) The Refrigerator and Its Influence on the Formation of the Political
    Ideology of the Ukrainian Emigration – B. Zorych
c) The Refrigerator as a Consolidating Factor of Canadian Women:
    Toward a History of the Women's movement in Canada – O. Kovbel
d) The Refrigerator as an Inexhaustible Source of Vital Optimism
    (Psychoanalytic Reflections) – Ya. Zorych
e) How We Acquired the Refrigerator (An Historical and Informative
    Study) – O. Malanchuk
f) The Deluxe '53 Model in the Light of the Most Recent Achievements of
    Contemporary Refrigeratorology and Cleanerism* – R. Malanchuk
g) "My Own Dear Refrigerator" – Recitation by Maria Malanchuk

10. Grandiose banquet accompanied by an informal friendly exchange on the subject of the newest brands of refrigerators, their models, prices, etc.

Free entry! No collection!

ОЛЬГА, МАРІЯ і РОМАН МАЛАНЧУКИ

мають шану запросити

ВАШУ ВСЕЧЕСНІСТЬ
на

ВЕЛИЧАВЕ РОДИННЕ СВЯТО

яке відбудеться в понеділок, 12 жовтня 1953 р., о год. 6 веч.,
в їхніх сальонах (191,Маркгам) з нагоди купна власного

РЕФРИДЖЕРЕЙТОРА

(марка „McClary", модель „Deluxe 1953", 7,6 куб. спеціяль-
ний „Butter Conditioner" з окремим регулятором темпера-
тури, ціна ... (?) — несподіванка для гостей).

ПРОГРАМА:
1. Святочне відкриття рефриджерейтора.
2. Торжественна мовчанка.
3. Урочисте проголошення ціни рефриджерейтора.
4. Ще торжественніша мовчанка.
5. Оплески.
6. Ґратуляції.
7. Привіти.
8. Овації.
9. Цикл академічних доповідей:
   a) Рефриджерейтор і збільшення консумпції пива, як головне завдання новоканадійців — Дост. Ю. Карманія.
   б) Рефриджерейтор і його вплив на формування політичної ідеології української еміграції — Б. Зорич.
   в) Рефриджерейтор як чинник об'єднуючий канадійське жіноцтво (До історії жінруху в Канаді) — О. Ковбель.
   г) Рефриджерейтор як певниче єдине джерело життєвого оптимізму (Психоаналітичні рефлексії) — Я. Зорич.
   ґ) Як ми здобули рефриджерейтор? (Історично - довідкова студія) — О. Маланчук.
   д) Модель „Deluxe 53" в світлі найновіших досягнень сучасної рефриджерейторології і кінерознавства — Р. Маланчук.
6. Мій рідний рефриджерейтор — декл. Доня Маланчук.
7. Грандіозний (від слова ґранда) бенкет, получений з товариською гутіркою на тему найновіших марок рефриджерейторів, їхніх моделів, цін тощо.

Вступ вільний! Нема колекти!

The original program in Ukrainian

*At this time, many Ukrainians immigrants spoke very little English. Regardless of their education, they were pleased to obtain work as janitors, office cleaners, or domestic cleaners, as this work provided an income that fed their families and paid for their housing. It was a very humble life, but it was a way to get settled and work toward a better future. The term cleanerism is a made-up word, but is used here as a recognition of the importance of the work that provided many people with a livelihood.

Olha Malanchuk holding Maria as a baby. At five years of age,
Maria was able to recite a poem, written by her father, on the grand occasion
of their purchase of an electric refrigerator.

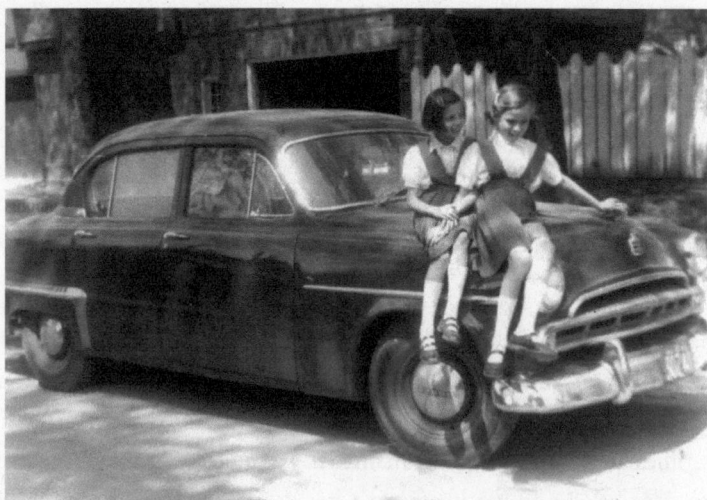

My sister and I sitting on my father's splendid green Desoto.

* * *

English is a very difficult language to master. There are so many irregularities. And then there is the pronunciation of certain words or phrases. The th sound was particularly difficult for my parents and their friends. Certain sounds were simply impossible to recreate. Most of the Ukrainian adults I knew did learn to speak English well, though almost all of them had an Eastern European accent.

My father never learned to speak English. He could blurt out a few phrases perfectly. For example, pulling into a service station to fill the car up with gas, he would open the window and say, "Good morning, sir. Fill her up, and check the oil, please." That phrase was perfectly said and eloquently expressed. No wonder the employees thought he could speak proper English. Of course, if they asked him a question, he was lost, and would turn to me and say, "What could he possibly want from me?" If he needed a translator, his friends would help.

That he never progressed beyond a few phrases baffled me, as he also knew Latin, and spoke German and Polish. He managed well, because the car mechanics often spoke German, and Polish was commonly used in the small deli shops on College and Bloor Streets. I never discussed the language issue with him, but I did wonder whether or not the war, the prison sentences, and the losses had simply been too much for him.

* * *

One of the first pieces of furniture the Malanchuks bought was an oak bookcase. It was to hold all their precious and valuable books. It was a large bookcase with glass doors that opened in the centre. The glass doors were blocked off in six-inch beveled glass squares. An old-fashioned key locked the bookcase and kept their beloved books safe.

The bookcase now stands in my eldest daughter Kvitka's living room, filled with her books. Maria now lives in Paris, France and used to work for the EU. The bookcase was of sentimental value, and she wanted it housed with friends who would appreciate and look after it. Taking the bookcase back to Paris was not an option.

Maria arrived in Paris to study French at the Sorbonne, and she is fluent in Ukrainian, French, and English. One of her first work experiences was working for the Shevchenko Scientific Society in Sarcelles, which published the Encyclopaedia of Ukraine in Ukrainian and then in English in conjunction with the Institute of Ukrainian Studies (Edmonton).[2] Subsequently, she worked for the French government as a trilingual translator. She is well informed about the political reality in Ukraine and has kept me abreast of events through articles, websites, and videos on a regular basis.

Maria was my mother's beloved god-daughter, and they had much in common. Ukrainian literature and the country's fate were of keen interest to them both. Topics such as what could be done about the plight of Ukrainian dissenters would absorb them in long and intense conversations.

I chat with Maria from time to time. It is good for me to hear elegant and proper Ukrainian expressed with a spirited voice. I listen carefully to the language I spoke so well as a young person. It's amazing how quickly a language suffers if it is not used frequently. My German is gone and my Ukrainian is disappearing. I have regrets.

---

2   Shevchenko Scientific Society, *Ukraine: A Concise Encyclopaedia* (Toronto: University of Toronto Press, 1971).

Looking Good Is a Chore

We were a family of four: mother, father, my younger sister, and me. From a very early age, my sister, Kvitka, was going to Hollywood. She was going to be a celebrity. She was going to be a big star.

Kvitka and her friend, Natalia, would sing and dance for hours at a time. They did have talent. Both were very musical, and they sang all their songs in harmony, but only my sister was driven by the call to fame. Come Hell or high water, Kvitka was going to be famous. This crusade for fame started early, perhaps at twelve years of age. Soon she had a repertoire of musical routines she practised regularly.

Hollywood was bound to discover her and provide her with her rightful place among the stars. I watched all this with a fair amount of scornfulness, and as I was two years older, I felt all her efforts were futile. I knew no one would discover her—certainly, no Hollywood agent would even know about this musical talent, singing and dancing on the second floor of our rooming house on Bathurst Street in Toronto.

To my horror, Kvi, as I called her, felt she had a disadvantage: me. I was the problem. How could she possibly be famous when her older sister looked like an unmade bed most days? Something had to be done.

When I think back to her determination, I am incredulous that she found a way to recreate her older sister's appearance. Somewhere, she saw an advertisement for tall, thin, young girls to apply to Walther Thornton's Modelling School on Avenue Road just north of Bloor Street. But her interest was focused on the ad's other offering: a self-improvement course that promised to turn shy and potentially awkward young girls into confident, graceful, and beautiful creatures. Here it was: a solution to her problem. Fix Chrystyna, and Hollywood would welcome Kvi with open arms. After all, she came from beautiful stock: the whole family would now be beautiful.

The amazing thing is that she managed to convince my parents that I needed this course, and that I was insecure and didn't know how to dress or act in social situations. I'm not sure why my parents bought into this. I wasn't beautiful, but I wasn't a wallflower, and I certainly knew how to talk to our family friends and neighbours. Actually, I thought I was well liked—perhaps not as popular as my friends, but quite content to be who I was.

My parents paid for the self-improvement course, and off I went for my sessions at Walther Thornton Modelling School. The courses were fun, but all this attention to colours, hairdos, proper makeup ... well that was good-to-know stuff, but I sure wasn't going to spend the time it all required. But my parents paid a lot for the course, so I had to make an effort to look as if I was going to change my ways.

I was told my hips were too wide, so each day, I would go down to the basement and practice corrective exercises suggested by the modelling school. I would bang each hip fifty times, twice a day on the cement floor. My parents thought this was a real effort on my part, though they were confused why I needed to do it.

I was not allowed to wear makeup to school, which was a big relief. But I did start to pay some attention to my wardrobe, and that appeased my sister. The course ended with a photography session. It took a few hours, with a variety of outfit changes. The big surprise was that I was photogenic. So, at the end of the course, I had a collection of photos in a variety of poses and outfits that did not look like me at all. I took the portfolio home and hid it.

Years later, I was cleaning out my desk and came across the portfolio. I looked at it, laughed at the memory, and was going to throw it out. My youngest, Zoja, who, very much like her aunt Kvitka, has a love of fashion, art, good meals, and gracious living, said "What's that?" She looked at it. "Give it to me, I know what to do with this." I had no idea what she planned.

That Christmas, Zoja's gifts consisted of nicely framed pictures of her mom as a sixteen-year-old, coiffed, painted up, and dressed to kill, posing in ways that were never her style or would ever be. But the pictures make them laugh, and the three girls have displayed them in their living rooms.

In one house, the photo even served a purpose.

I have always been concerned about feeding my children well. That concern extended to my first grandchild. It was a worry, and I fretted over everyone's eating habits. My grandson, two years old, picked up on that worry. One morning, when he had polished off all his porridge, he ran to get my fancy picture, and placed it in front of his bowl. His mother Larissa (my middle child) was intrigued watching him. He looked at my picture, pointed to his empty bowl, and said, "Look, Nana, all gone!"

One of the pictures taken during the photography session of the course.

Mr. Levytsky

Myron Levytsky was a member of the anti-mosquito brigade, where his colourful behaviour was reminiscent of a naughty school boy. He arrived to Canada with the reputation of a recognised and accomplished artist in Ukraine. Subsequently, he became a respected, celebrated and much sought-after artist in Canada and internationally.

In the article "Fifty Creative Years" in the monograph entitled Myron Levytsky, Daria Darewych, an art historian and professor of art history, wrote the following:

> Myron Levytsky, who exhibits under the name Lev, is the most popular living Ukrainian painter in Canada and one of the most prominent Ukrainian artists working outside Ukraine. His widespread reputation stems from hundreds of books he has designed and illustrated since 1935, from several hundred oil paintings and prints, as well as the ten churches he has painted in Ukraine, Canada and Australia.[3]

Myron Levytsky had a profound influence on our upbringing. My sister and I had no idea of the significance of this man's talent in our community. We simply regarded him as one would a favoured uncle. As we matured, we realised that our family friend was an admired and acknowledged artist.

In the 1950s, most of us, new arrivals, lived in downtown Toronto. While Levytsky's first wife and child lived on the third floor of our house, Levytsky had a studio down the street from us on Bathurst, where he lived and painted.

---

3   Daria Darewych, *Myron Levytsky* (Toronto: Ukrainian Artists' Association, 1985), 18.

We saw him almost every day when he came to visit his child. Both he and his wife were devoted to their child, a beautiful little boy named Marko.

Levytsky visited his son and us on a daily basis. We loved to see him. He was a positive influence on my parents, who, at times, could be far too rigid. He had a wonderful sense of humour and constantly used it to amuse or to deflate tense situations.

Marko was a delightful young child, and we were all very fond of him. He roamed the house, and as our first tenants were Ukrainian, he could move from one family to another with ease. One day, my mother was up on the third floor, chatting to someone, and realised she had to rush downstairs, as she was expecting Pani Zelena (Mrs. Green) to come for tea.

Having overheard the conversation, Marko was fascinated that a green person was coming to the house. As soon as the doorbell rang, he rushed downstairs and into the kitchen to get a good view of this lady. His initial great expectation quickly turned into a huge disappointment. There was no green lady—only a rather ordinary looking person. He stood in the kitchen, totally perplexed, and finally blurted out, "Excuse me, excuse me, but where is the green lady?" My mother finally noticed him, and it took her some time to try and explain why her friend was not green.

"But where is the green lady?" became a common phrase in our household whenever something was not what it was supposed to be. We simply would respond to the dilemma with, "But where is the green lady?"

Levytsky was the only person in our community who could get away with behaviour no one else dared. He had affairs—probably quite a few. But he was discreet, and would try to mislead the gossipers. I do remember my father's amusement as he recounted an evening's function at the community hall. In came Myron Levytsky, with his wife on one arm and another attractive woman on the other. My father leaned over to his friend and said, "How does he do it? They would crucify us if any one of us tried to make that kind of an entrance."

His friend replied, "Well, Misko," (one of my father's nicknames) "you have to be an artiste" (he emphasised the French word in order to give it more flair) "to get away with that."

Regardless, Levytsky was great fun. After visiting his wife and child upstairs, he would appear in our kitchen and offer to help with our homework. He

enjoyed doing the drawings assigned in various subjects. It was not excep-
tional art—a few strokes and it was done—but what we handed in was far
better than most of the other students' work. Often, he would amuse himself
and interpret a subject with a bit of humour. My biology notebook was full
of remarkable drawings. I certainly did not deserve the marks I received for
my so-called efforts. I justified my marks by thinking the art was just a bonus
and that, really, the content had been the important thing.

For young students, our community held dances. On festive occasions,
there were more elaborate dances, with dinner and a live orchestra. The whole
family came to these events, dressed in their finest from tip to toe. Since few
could afford to buy outfits, most dresses were made by our mothers. My
mother made most of our clothes in elementary school, but in high school
Mrs. B made our clothes.

She was an amazing seamstress, made her own patterns and could produce
an outfit that was simply fabulous. I did have one disappointment. She made
a lovely skirt for me, exactly what I had wanted, but it looked bland on me.
Mr. Levytsky came to the rescue: "Give me that skirt. Let's see what I can do
with this." He spread it out on the table and, within minutes, came back with
a box of coloured paints and decorated the skirt by creating a flower border
around the hem. All of a sudden I had an amazing skirt. The skirt and I went
to the dance, looking pretty smug and happy.

Another time, a pink taffeta number was dolled up by pulling the skirt
up a bit and attaching a hand-made fabric rose of the same material. I don't
remember all his efforts on our behalf, but he brought a lot of colour and joy
into our lives.

When I was fifteen, Levytsky painted portraits of my sister and me. They
were considered very modern pieces of art. At that age, I did not appreciate
the work, but now it hangs on my living room wall and I love it. The portrait
does not look like me. Rather, it is a representation of who I was: a very
serious, introverted soul. It may have been me then, but it certainly isn't me
now. I think Levytsky found me a challenge. He often implied I needed more
frivolity in my life. He, of course, was an expert on the subject.

One day, he arrived and announced that I needed to accompany him to
the Toronto Art Gallery. I wasn't particularly interested in art, but he took me

to a Van Gogh exhibition, and that visit changed my view of art. It certainly was an awakening to the power and beauty someone can create on a canvas.

The colours were dazzling, and the composition of the pieces took my breath away. I asked a friend of mine, Katharine Dagg, a Charlottetown painter, what it was that people found addictive in Van Gogh's work. She explained how Van Gogh dragged his paintbrush, thick with paint, over the canvas until the paint broke up and the light came through his work. It was his ability to use the technique of thick brush strokes that manipulated the light in his work.

She also pointed out that Van Gogh limited the number of colours he used in each painting to achieve intensity. He preferred bold colours, often making use of complementary colours or tonal variations of the same colour. The lighter parts of a painting tended to be thicker, with broken brush strokes or even the use of pointillism. Dark colours were applied more thinly and had a sheen, to create a contrast of light and shadow. These were Katharine Dagg's comments on Van Gogh, which she pointed out to me on my front porch.

I don't remember Levytsky's lecture on Van Gogh. All I know is I was and am still hooked on appreciating the visual pleasures of this world. It's a mystery to me that it took me so long to discover the joy art gives us, and how it educates us through, its visual interpretation of events in our lives.

My mother loved her books and her art collection. She purchased paintings whenever she could afford it. As a respected Ukrainian editor, she edited books, biographies, autobiographies, pamphlets, and anything the artists or writers (and others) in our community needed. Her fee was always marginal—she enjoyed the work and was often paid in kind. That pleased her even more than money.

I have inherited wonderful paintings. Often, I sit in my living room, admiring the treasures that hang on my wall. I feel so privileged to have some of my mother's collection. It's a great gift.

Levytsky was particular about to whom he sold his works. Customers did not always leave with a painting. One day, he told us he was expecting a serious buyer the following afternoon. That afternoon ended, and he came along for his usual visit after speaking with his wife and child. We were anxious to hear his news. He said nothing. My mother finally asked him if he had sold anything. He admitted that he hadn't. My mother knew something was not right, and slowly pried it out of him. He did not like the couple of buyers, and the longer they stayed, the less he liked them. He was convinced that they were buying only because he was popular in the Ukrainian community and they would be able to say they owned one of his oils. The couple was Ukrainian, and well known for their deep pockets. By this time, he really was quite a famous artist.

So the doomed couple would indicate a painting of interest to them and Levytsky would say, "I'm so sorry, this one is promised to someone else," or that he was planning to give the painting to a friend. In short, whatever they found interesting was not for sale. In a room full of paintings, nothing was available.

My mother, who knew him very well, asked him whether it wasn't time for him to buy a new jacket as he had been wearing the one he paraded around in for a very long time. He did admit that money was an issue, but felt a new jacket would just have to wait.

"Wait?! You wouldn't have to wait if you sold a few of your works!" she scolded him.

"But—but—but I am very attached to this jacket. How can I appreciate a new jacket if I don't appreciate the one I own? Don't expect me to discard something that has served me so well and for so long!" he blurted out.

My mother was speechless, then started to laugh. "Really, Myrontsio," (a diminutive) "you can be so annoying."

The truth was he was able to earn enough money as an artist to support his wife, child, and himself. His art was in great demand, and he did very well in the following years. He did acquire quite a few new jackets, and wore them with flair.

One evening, he marched into our kitchen and started pacing around the room. My mother wanted to know what the problem was. He looked at her and said, "I don't understand. I finally have an elegant new jacket on, and nobody has noticed it!" We burst out laughing. What a faux pas on our part.

Years later, when I was about to marry, my mother talked Levytsky into painting an icon for me. Levytsky was knowledgeable in Ukrainian religious art and had already painted the interior of many churches. I loved the icon he painted for me, and it inspired me to collect others. I now have a wall of icons painted by a variety of Ukrainian artists, some of whom I knew personally, others who were acquaintances of my parents. All of them are dead now, but the icons live on and provide me with some spiritual comfort. I am not a religious person and neither was Levytsky, but he knew a great deal about our religion and knew how to represent it, as a connection to Ukrainian traditions and culture. It's hard to imagine how one would separate them. Religion, traditions, and our culture are intertwined in a tight weave. Pull on a thread and you could unravel the lot.

Take for example, the pagan aspects of our culture, which still pop up in Christmas carols, Easter songs, and in our famous Easter eggs—in which one can see a representation of both pagan and religious Christian symbols, displayed as one. In Christmas carols, there may be a reference to the sun god, and in the next verse, one would be glorifying the birth of the baby Jesus. There are special Easter songs called hahilky, where again, there may be a reference to Lada, the spring goddess, and, in the same song, to Christ rising from the dead.

Levytsky was well versed in all these things and could answer any of my questions about the symbols or colours in his religious art. My wedding icon has Mary in a red cape, not blue. He explained to me that red was the colour of Mary's cape in the Eastern rite. Regardless of the colour of her cape, I love my icon, and when I look at her, she reminds me of my parents' effort to arrive in a safe and free country in which they would have the ability to provide us with a worthwhile, fortunate life.

I have five oils by Levytsky and two prints. I had a lovely watercolour of Levytsky's favourite haunts in Paris. I told him how much I liked it, and he took it off his wall and gave it to me. When my daughter Larissa graduated from the Nova Scotia College of Art and Design, she indicated how much she liked the painting. It now hangs on her wall. I know Levytsky would have loved my daughter, and it would have pleased him that I gave it to her.

My interest in art comes mainly from my mother, who treasured her collection, but Levytsky is the man who enriched my interest in art. If ever I should find myself in dire need, I'd sell every piece of my furniture before I'd sell any piece of art. It's not worth a fortune, but it's worth a plethora of memories—one cannot give those up. Like Levytsky, I'd sooner give it away to deserving friends than put a price tag on it.

Myron Levytsky died in 1993. He was such a constant figure in our lives—part of our family, really. Like a favourite uncle, with a few liberal ideas on how life should be lived. What a lucky perk, to have an eccentric, dramatic, colourful intellectual to balance my parents' well-meaning but, at times, rigid ways.

My parents did not always agree with him, but they had a very close and warm friendship. He was always welcome in our home.

* * *

Levytsky very quietly managed to save my wedding day. My parents were not pleased with the person with whom I wished to spend the rest of my life. He wasn't Ukrainian. They liked him as a person, but not as my husband. My mother tried everything to make me change my mind. First, there was the bribe of an all-expenses paid trip to Europe, where friends of the family would ensure I had a grand time. That didn't work, so then, my mother tried using her type of logic to encourage me to rethink what I was about to do. She would say to me, "Why marry? Be a teacher, cook for no one, go to the opera on the weekends, travel in the summer. Do as you wish. Why compromise your lifestyle for a man? Be your own boss!" When all failed, she announced, "Marry him and you will have a husband who will never understand your Slavic soul!"

Even my sister got into the act by saying, "Oh my God, you want to marry a Maritimer? Don't you know they wear white socks with everything?"

The *Toronto Star* had done a feature article called "White Socks from the Maritimes." We had read that feature quite a few years before, but as the family fashionista, she would remember that feature many years later.

Levytsky pulled me aside and told me that in our tradition, the bride bought the wedding bands. Not having been married before, I was not aware of that obligation. I had twenty dollars in my purse, and on the day of my wedding, I walked up to Bloor Street to pick up my dress and to find two wedding rings so I could get married. I entered the first jewellery store and the man behind the counter could tell I was distressed. There was nothing I could afford. He asked me how he could help me.

I didn't know how to begin, and finally blurted out that I needed two gold rings, one for me and one for my future husband, whom I was to marry that morning. "And this is all the money I have," I said as I pulled out a crumpled bill out of my purse. He didn't miss a beat, saying, "Well, this is your lucky day. I have two gold rings for twenty dollars. They're just plain, but they'll do the trick for you." I couldn't believe my luck! I thanked him and ran home with the rings and the dress, fairly confident that all was going to be well. Surely, this wedding would go ahead as planned.

I didn't realise that there were more hurdles to overcome. Levytsky supported me and tried to alleviate my parents' feelings of despair. He did two more things to save the wedding day. I did not have a maid of honour, as my sister, being married, could not be one. Of course, there was no one else, as my parents had insisted it was to be a family affair, with no guests invited. Levytsky stepped in and said, "No problem, I'll stand for her." The priest looked perplexed as Levytsky pointed out that there was nothing in our tradition that didn't allow a male to step in to save the day. Besides, all the Ukrainian priests knew who Levytsky was, a respected and renowned painter of the interior of Ukrainian Greek Catholic Churches. Few would question his judgement.

Then, there was the problem of the wreaths. I forgot that the bride and groom are crowned with wreaths during the wedding ceremony. There were no wreaths, and my mother was delighted. No wreaths, no wedding, she thought. Again, Levytsky came to the rescue. He took my bouquet, pulled out the greenery, and produced two wreaths, lickety-split.

Eventually, the wedding took place, though my husband claims he has no idea whether he's married or not. He did not understand a word that was spoken. But the cheap gold ring has stayed on his finger through the many years we have been together.

The wedding party was very small and uncommon: my parents, Mr. and Mrs. Holman, my sister and her husband, Levytsky, and Nancy White, Alan's cousin. Henry Phillips was to be the best man, but he was delayed when he tried to return from the States, so Nancy did the honours. A very unorthodox wedding, to say the least. After the wedding ceremony, there was a meal at our house. Alan and I left shortly after the meal for Prince Edward Island, but the rest of them stayed.

My parents did have a change of heart—especially after the first grandchild was born. Unfortunately, my father died early, on March 12, 1984. He was seventy-one years old. In his last few years, he was weak and in need of care—his health failed him. His humour did not.

Eventually, my mother learned to appreciate my husband. He was kind to her. He liked her, and he liked the way she was able to rattle off her insults without hesitation. She was also a well-read and well-informed woman with whom one could have a serious discussion.

One of my guests reported to me that Levytsky had had too much to drink at the wedding. I hardly blame him, as he had worked hard to save my wedding and, at the same time, not annoy my parents. He apparently made several passes at Nancy and my mother-in-law. Two months later, I was back in Toronto, and as was my habit, I went to see him. He had moved to an apartment on the third floor on Bathurst Street, near Dupont. He was living there with his mistress. Eventually, he married her.

I rang the doorbell, and down he came to open the door. He was so pleased to see me. "Oh, it's so good to see you. Come up, come up to the apartment. This calls for freshly roasted coffee. I'll just run around the corner and get the beans." Which he did. He ground the beans and produced a really wonderful, strong cup of coffee. He bombarded me with questions. How was I getting along? How different was my new life? Did I have any regrets? And so on.

Finally, I looked at him and asked, "Mister Levytsky, at the wedding, did you really make a pass at my new mother-in-law, Mrs. Holman?"

"Oh," he said, "I had no choice. I did not want your father to disgrace himself, so better me than him." We knew that he loved women—all kinds. He was a terrible flirt. He was also very kind and eager to help us look our best. Anyone who asked his advice received sincere and appropriate suggestions.

Despite his antics, he was adored by my family. My mother had started a trend in our community. As Levytsky was painting my wedding gift, people who came into the studio were impressed and reminded of how an icon was a traditional wedding gift in Ukraine. The tradition in Slavic countries is for icons to be given as presents to bless the newlyweds. Also, an icon made an appropriate gift for a new home.

Orders came in, and after painting quite a few icons, Myron Levytsky said to my mother, "What have you begun? I have too many orders for Virgin Mary icons as wedding gifts for young women. You should know that I am getting very tired of painting the Holy Virgin for young women who are in all probability not virgins."

My parents' wedding gift to me. The icon was painted by Myron Levytsky.

My portrait, which now hangs on my living room wall, painted by Myron Levytsky.

МИРОН ЛЕВИЦЬКИЙ
MYRON LEVYTSKY
1913-1993

Photo of Myron Levytsky

Mrs. C

My mother's business sense was a surprise. She managed to build up a cleaning business relatively quickly. I do not know where she got the idea, but it did help us financially—rather nicely. As soon as we acquired the house for ourselves, she opened the cleaning business in the front room. At first, she ran it herself and her English improved remarkably as she dealt with customers. People liked her. She had a good sense of humour, and she amused herself by having short discussions with her customers. This gave her a good perspective of the neighbourhood in which we lived.

One night, our doorbell rang at 2 a.m.—the middle of the night. I heard my mother open the door to find a woman with whom she only had a nodding acquaintance. She was dressed in her nightgown and her housecoat and was holding a small suitcase. She had had an argument with her family and had no place to go. She was frightened and did not want to spend the night on the street. Physical and verbal abuse by family members was not common, but it did happen. She sounded heartbroken. My mother brought her into the kitchen so she could listen to her story. Eventually, my mother fixed up a bed for her and that is how she came to live with us.

Mrs. C was given a small room on the third floor. It was a pleasant room with a bed, a dresser, and a chair on which she could sit and read her newspapers. There were cooking facilities in the basement, though there was also a hotplate in her room. She may have shared our kitchen at times. It was a very loose arrangement. She often ate with us or cooked for us—my memory is not clear on this. However, she became part of our family, and we treated her as such. My sister and I liked her. She was nice to us and we were always respectful of her. I don't remember ever hearing a harsh word from her. I couldn't imagine why she was put out by her family.

When Mrs. C came to live with us, besides her small suitcase, she was allowed to retrieve her old portable Singer machine from home. This machine used a hand crank and did not require an electrical outlet. It could be put anywhere. It was conveniently placed on a small table. Mrs. C could sew, and mother noticed that there were quite a few customers who needed some alterations on one thing or another. Many of the customers were young university students who were forever losing buttons on their clothes. There was a need in the neighbourhood for this kind of service. Besides, Mrs. C needed a job, and she could do far more than sew on buttons. You could hear the little Singer machine sing as it mended all kinds of outfits.

Mrs. C did a superb job, and the business grew. She became well known in the neighbourhood as the woman with a big heart and low fees. The university students caught on quickly and brought in their alterations. When they would sigh deeply and share with her how much they missed their mothers, they paid nothing. Mrs. C would never charge someone whose mother was not there to help them. No amount of lecturing or reasoning by my mother made any difference. It was her time and her money—end of discussion.

It really made no difference to us, but knowing how little she had, we watched how quickly she shared her earnings with those more needy than her. Mrs. C was lucky—if she gave something away, sure enough, someone would come in and give her something she could use.

She had a yellow cardigan she loved. One day, a young mother came into the shop with her baby. She was dressed in very flimsy clothes. Mrs. C took off her beloved cardigan and gave it to her. My mother chastised her for giving away her only cardigan, but she did not seem to care. Two days later, she came waltzing into the kitchen with quite a splendid sweater someone had given her that morning. How pleased she was to reverse the lecture and tell my mother that good deeds are always rewarded!

The business was so successful that it was time to move it to a better location. Also, it was useful for us to reclaim the living room. Where to put the business was the question. So, mother decided that since there was a door to the basement facing the side street, she would hire someone to dig out the basement floor and make a room with enough height, which would be accessible through the side door. This huge project took a long time to complete. When it was finished, it looked quite professional, with a proper counter, a sewing table, and a solid bar attached to the ceiling upon which the various cleaned outfits were hung.

Mrs. C was ecstatic—it was her business now, and she served her customers with pleasure. Though her English was limited, she managed, as she spoke German and Polish fluently, in addition to Ukrainian.

Our house on Bathurst Street became a busy place. Down in the basement, Mrs. C ran the cleaning business, working her magic with her trusty sewing machine, which now had its own table on which to sit. You could hear her dealing with customers, enjoying the exchanges and learning about the people in the neighbourhood.

We also had a second business running out of the basement by an elderly gentleman, Mr. V, who had been a tailor in Ukraine. He set up shop next to Mrs. C's new and updated cleaning business. His business relied only on Ukrainian customers, as his English was almost non-existent. I don't think he had a lot of customers, but the work gave him a reason to get up in the morning and get himself to our place. So whether there was work or not, the basement was a place where one could pop in and have a chat with either of these two good people. And pop in they did. The side door was always unlocked—one did not have to ring the main doorbell to get in, and most of the time, we did not care who was visiting in the basement.

There was a wonderful old gas stove close to Mr. V's work table so he and Mrs. C could make coffee or tea for their visitors. It was a combination of a work area and a social gathering place.

My father loved the social gatherings down in the basement. He would come home from work and have someone to talk to and discuss the goings-on in the community. These were not rowdy occasions—just times when a friend or two needed a chat, a little sympathy, or to hear a joke.

Mr. V was not in good health. His daughter was a close friend of my mother's. I think the two of them concocted this idea of giving her father a place to go that he could call work and so he could have something to do. Mr. V was a well-liked man and people came in just to see him.

I remember he had a good sense of humour. One little story he told was about bumping into an old friend. He was walking down Spadina Street, a street full of clothing outlets, when he was embraced by a fellow with a Yiddish accent. The man said, "Petre, Petre, I thought you were dead ... but you're alive! We're both alive! We both survived the war! Isn't it wonderful?!" They had both been tailors in Lviv, and Mr. V was amused and delighted that his old pal recognised him. I liked that story. It was a happy ending for two lives that reconnected in Canada.

When the war broke out, Mrs. C fled to Canada with her family and times became very tough. Unfortunately, her husband took it out on her. A nasty piece of business, he was. She remained with us even after we sold the house and the business and moved to Etobicoke, a suburb west of Toronto. She left us occasionally, when someone in the community needed a housekeeper. But she always had a room in our house. We knew she was kind, but she was also good company, well read and a subscriber to at least two newspapers—one in German and one in Polish. She could also read any of the Ukrainian newspapers that came to the house, and many did. She enjoyed reading the newspapers, wanting to be informed about local and world events.

When my parents told her they were moving, she was surprised to discover they intended to take her with them. My father made one request: "No more crying in the kitchen. You have cried enough for the poor, the sick, the wretched souls you have read about. Enough! We want you to be happy. You can cry to your heart's content in your room." The truth was he was very fond of her, and enjoyed their conversations.

Mrs. C had one treasured possession. It was an autographed picture of Queen Juliana of The Netherlands that had an inscription, which, according to my memory, said:

To Mrs. C, and her kind heart.
Affectionately,
HRH Queen Juliana

Mrs. C had read about a very sick child who needed a life-saving surgery available only in New York at the time. Apparently, the Queen had found out about this child's sad predicament and she paid for the surgery and all the costs. According to the newspaper story, the Queen then flew to New York to see how the child was doing. This last piece of the article was a description of a gesture that truly impressed our Mrs. C. She could not stop talking about it. So, she took pen to paper and wrote Queen Juliana a rather touching letter. The Queen thanked Mrs. C for her kind words and included an auto-graphed photograph of herself.

I may not have all the pieces right, but I do know how very proud Mrs. C was of her photo of her friend, HRH Queen Juliana of the Netherlands. She derived much pleasure from displaying it in the most prominent spot in her room.

As a young girl, I felt very confused about Mrs. C. I could not believe that anyone living in Canada could have so little. All her possessions could fit into a small suitcase. So, when she occasionally moved to be someone's housekeeper, she would be packed and ready to go in a few minutes.

* * *

Mrs. C had an unexpected dramatic flair. When my parents moved to Etobicoke, she acquired a new role. My mother was forever busy at her typewriter, organising community events, writing speeches for herself and for others. Her big challenge was to prepare the quarterly international maga-zine Ukrainian Woman's World and have it ready for publishing. She was both the editor of the magazine and the national secretary for the National Council of the Ukrainian Women's Organisation of Canada. Her work and commitment to this organisation began early, in 1950.

I often helped her put the magazine together. It had to be ready for an offset press. We glued the articles, photos, and recipes onto the pages. Often, there were gaps. But mother had a knack for filling in small empty spaces. Poetry was her big saviour. She could whip up a poem to fill a space, no problem. Or she would paste in a picture of a piece of embroidery or an art motif. She signed her poetry "Anonymous," but many readers knew who the "unknown" was. There wasn't usually much argument about the layout of the magazine, though her patience would sometimes be tested, as certain contributors insisted that their piece be placed in the top left-hand corner of the page: the best and most prominent place.

Recipes were her downfall. She was sloppy with these contributions: some of them lacked clarity. If the recipe didn't quite fit the page, she took out parts of the instructions. She rationalised that the basics were there, and the frivolous stuff could go. To be fair, this did not happen often.

The magazine always included a page of Ukrainian recipes, many of which were quite good and sent in by cooks from coast to coast who lived mostly in Canada. Occasionally, I would point out her lack of complete instructions for a recipe.

I tried baking a torte once, which called for a can of pineapple. I followed the recipe closely, and my torte was a sopping mess. I called my mother.

"That can of pineapple in the recipe - do I have to drain it?" My mother sighed and said, "Of course ... any idiot would know that you drink the juice and use the pulp." Well, this idiot didn't know that. I did not bother to point out that the recipe would be perfect if these details had not been dropped from the write-up.

A reproduction of a Woman's World cover by Myron Levytsky as featured in the book by Daria Darewych.[4]

---

4   Daria Darewych, *Myron Levytsky*. (Toronto: Ukrainian Artists' Association, 1985), 14.

Woman's World cover: Young girls in Ukrainian costumes dancing and singing Easter songs called Hahilky, by Halyna Mazepa—a famous Ukrainian artist who lived in Caracas, Venezuela. My mother edited her biography.[5]

Now, Mrs. C was a huge supporter of my mother's. Regardless of her dramatic nature, Mrs. C. stood firmly in my mother's corner. In this new arrangement, she was often asked to answer the phone, whenever my mother had a project that had a pressing deadline. I was present once when Mrs. C had this assignment.

That day, mother had no time to talk to anyone. Perhaps because she was not able to deny anyone their requests. And there were many. Throughout her life, she belonged to a variety of organisations. She was an active member of Plast, the Ukrainian Scouting Movement, in addition to being principal of Toronto's Ukrainian high school and editor of Ukrainian Woman's World, to name a few. Mrs. C. knew how hard she worked and admired her for her commitment to others.

---

5   *Ukrainian Woman's World* 54, no. 12 (2003).

So, the phone often rang. This particular day, the phone rang constantly, and Mrs. C grew irritated by the interruptions. She answered it, and I could hear her agitated voice say, "Why don't you people leave Mrs. Z alone? She works from morning till night, and the phone never stops ringing. How is the poor woman able to finish her work when all you people keep ringing her? ... Yes, yes, I know, you need to talk to her. I'll tell her that you called."

Many times, after having heard who was calling, my mother would yell out, "It's OK, Mrs. C, I will speak to them." This would unsettle Mrs. C, and she would mutter under her breath, "Why does she do that? I tell them she is not available and she yells out that she is. I feel like a fool."

However uncomfortable it made Mrs. C, the arrangement where she would answer the phone went on for a long time. They seemed to put up with each other's shortcomings.

Mrs. C lived with us, on and off, for the rest of her life. The two women had a very good rapport, and discussed all sorts of situations. However, they never used their first names—that kind of familiarity wasn't accepted, especially since there was a significant age difference between them.

In many ways Mrs. C's life was a happy story. She was busy and productive. She was well regarded and well known for her kindness to others. Whenever I came to visit, she had stories to tell, seeing the humour in some very ordinary events. In most of her stories, she made fun of herself. Here's a favourite old story from our time on Bathurst Street:

Mrs. C was on the bus. The driver refused to wait for an elderly soul trying hard to catch it. People on the bus noticed, and a few tried to make the driver aware of the situation. He wouldn't wait. It was time for Mrs. C's stop. She marched to the front of the bus. While getting out, she loudly said to the driver, so all could hear her insult, "You, you very, very big porky pig!" She was so proud. Somewhere, she had heard the words "porky pig" and assumed that was a proper way to put someone in their place.

When she lived with us in Etobicoke, she had a part-time job in a clothing store, looking after the children's section. She liked to keep the clothes on her counter nicely folded and in good order. Some customers upset her, including a lady who came in and made a mess of the boys' pants, neatly folded and arranged by size. Mrs. C was not happy and pointed it out by saying, "Lady, lady, this no house, only pants."

Mrs. C could not understand why the woman had to mess up her tidy work. She said to me, "She wasn't buying a house. If she was buying a house then I could understand why she needed to inspect everything. She was only buying one pair of boys' pants." Then she muttered under her breath a profanity in Ukrainian, only to find out the woman understood her. Words were spoken. Fortunately, all ended well.

Fitting In

There were afternoon sessions when my father's friends would gather in our kitchen and philosophise about their existence, which would become more and more ridiculous as the bottle was emptied. These festive occasions would come to an abrupt halt as soon as my mother came home and threw all the participants out. I remember the feeble protests of my father's friends as they left, which had no impact on my mother. You could hear their pleas.

"But Slavusia," (a diminutive) "why do we have to leave? We were having such a serious discussion. We only sipped a few shot glasses of vodka. Really, this is painful. Here you are, a beauty in our midst, so heartlessly ending our pleasure."

None of this had any effect on my mother. Out they went—there was no other option for them. She was famous for her direct and unceremonious demands on my father's friends. Not one of them seemed to hold a grudge, as they always returned and joked about how the night would end. My mother was known for her quick-witted, sharp tongue and in a community where good lines were cherished, one was admired even by the folks who had just been insulted.

Roman and Olha Malanchuk were probably the closest friends my parents had. In the beginning, they lived with us on Bathurst Street, eventually moving on to a second-floor apartment on Markham Street. All of us were taken with their dark-eyed baby, Maria, whom we all called Donia (which means "daughter"). Children were often given nicknames, which were usually dropped as they reached adulthood.

The Malanchuks were Ukraine's intellectual elite, well-educated and very involved in various aspects of Ukrainian life. Olha Malanchuk, as I mentioned, was a trained teacher, and enjoyed working with young children, teaching them how to read and write. Owing to her great interpersonal skills, she was hired as general manager to the Ukrainian publishing company Vilne Slovo ("Free Word") in Toronto, which published a weekly newspaper and books. She handled disagreements with tact and kindness, and was successful at resolving most office disputes. She was a spirited soul who enjoyed adventures. When the Ontario government organised one-week trips for non-English-speaking publishers to tour Ontario in order to boost their impressions and knowledge of Canada, Olha Malanchuk volunteered to go up in a helicopter and cruise down rivers in a motorboat representing her company. Others from her workplace were not so brave. Her participation in that excursion earned her the name "Zhyttieradisna Pani Olha" and "Zhyttieradisna dama" ("Joyous in life Mrs. Olha" and "Joyous in life dame"). These were high compliments of her, by the staff and all of us.

When the family moved to New York, Olha Malanchuk worked as head of administration for Radio Svoboda ("Radio Liberty"). Maria, Olha, and Roman Malanchuk all volunteered for Smoloskyp (a non-profit publishing company) translating texts written by dissidents and smuggled out of the Gulags by brave women who had risked their lives to do so.

Before the war, Roman Malanchuk received his diploma in Law from the University of Vienna. He was politically active, and had served three prison sentences before the age of twenty-one. He worked as a journalist in a publishing house in Lviv, writing articles that were anti-Soviet, anti-Nazi, and anti-Polish. He was arrested by the Nazi SS and imprisoned in the Central Berlin prison, where he was tortured and so weakened by hunger that he could only crawl on all fours. The prison was bombed by the American air force, and when he saw the walls crumble before his eyes, he crawled out. He and Olha managed to find each other in war-torn Europe. They went to Genoa to travel to Canada. They boarded the ship SD Sturgis, where they met my parents.

In Canada, Malanchuk was regarded as a distinguished editor in the Ukrainian language. Very soon after settling in Toronto, he went back to school, mastered English, and received a degree in library science. He was one of the few Ukrainians of his generation who managed to work in his field. After he received a valid Canadian degree from the University of Ottawa, he was able to acquire a position with the Toronto Public Library heading up the Slavic section. Eventually, he was hired by the New York Public Library located on the corner of 5th Avenue and 42nd Street, as vice-head of the Slavonic section. Maria tells me he loved his work in New York. It was an impressive career. In addition, he made a number of contributions to scientific journals, political articles, reviews, works of fiction, and humorous commentary to accompany Levytsky's drawings in the satirical journal Komar. One of his major achievements was the annotated bibliography of V. Vynnychenko, who was a statesman, writer, and first prime minister of Ukraine. He published this biography under yet another, brand-new pseudonym.

Though he had a demanding career, he never lost his sense of humour or his gentle ways. I was extremely fond of him and Olha. Both played an integral part in my life. I knew they were extremely well-thought-of in our community, but for me, they were adults who always treated me as a special guest in their home. It was wonderful to have them in my life, as people who accepted me as the child I was.

Roman Malanchuk was someone we all loved to have come into the house. He usually entered through the back door, and we often heard him before we saw him. There was a window into the backyard, and he would stand under it and sing:

Everybody loves my baby
But my baby loves nobody but meeeee.

He would pull the last note for some time. It was a silly little ditty, and we thought it hilarious, and laughed as one of us ran to the back door to open it for him. This number didn't seem to have a melody—just a beat that was appealing. He came quite often and entertained us with stories of his youth, and then he and my father would spend the rest of the time discussing their new life in Canada.

There were four very close friends who often gathered in our kitchen and sat on our majestic green sofa. There was Roman Malanchuk, Myron Levytsky, and, occasionally, Borys Oleksandriv Hrybinsky, the poet (Oleksandriv was his pen-name, Hrybinsky was his surname). It was one of those afternoons, when the four of them were entertaining each other with stories, that I arrived home from university. I had gotten a lift from Kingston from a fellow who had a nice, comfortable car. He had driven me home a few times before. Not knowing who was in the house and because it was only the afternoon, I thought it would be polite to invite the fellow in for a cup of tea. So in we went.

Now, when you walked in, the living room was to the left. The two rooms that had become the dining room and my parents' bedroom had a long, dark corridor that skirted around the rooms and led to the kitchen. As I passed the living room and entered the corridor, I heard them and I simply froze. I had no idea how to explain to my friend who they were and what they were doing in the kitchen. So, on I went, with this poor fellow behind me.

As we entered the kitchen, I knew instantly that I could never explain what was going on, nor could I justify the scene. The four were standing, glasses in hand, listening to one of them propose a toast. The toast proposed, all four downed their drinks and started to fill up their glasses again, when they noticed us. Then, all four looked pleased.

"Who is this?" said my father. I explained he was a friend from school. He looked at the fellow and said, "A university student, oh good! He'll have a drink with us?" I translated. My friend looked horrified, and said he could not have a drink so early in the day. The four men looked bewildered. My father turned to his friends and said, "Do you understand this? What university student did we ever know who would refuse a drink? Let's see," (a pause, obviously scheming a solution,) "we'll have a toast in English. A toast no Canadian student will be able to refuse."

And so, the game began. I don't remember all the toasts, but all were refused, making my friend very uncomfortable. Finally, one of the four said, "I know, I know, we'll toast the Queen. Surely he'll drink to her." Up they got, and one of them said in English, "Gentlemen, a toast, to her Royal Highness, Queen Elizabeth the Second." They offered a glass to my friend. At this point, the fellow turned and charged out of the house. I said I was sorry, offering tea was awkward, but he did not seem to hear me. He did not accept my apology, and he was gone. He never offered to drive me home again.

I returned to the kitchen. My father was in full swing. "Who did you bring home? That fellow has no sense of decorum or civilised behaviour.

What would you want with him? Try and bring home someone with some flair, some interest in having a good time. Forget him—the kitchen doorknob is more interesting than him."

And so it went on and on, all four encouraging me to socialise more with young men of a certain calibre, not boring people like the fellow who had just left. I had to swear I was not interested in him. I was only interested in his car, because it was quite grand and he never charged me. (Though I did buy the coffee and sweets on the way home.) If you think I impressed them with my logic, I did not. Thankfully, at that point, my mother returned home. I was saved from another lecture from the four as they were unceremoniously dispatched home by her, and the fun ended.

Another explanation of the men's behaviour was that these were men who had lived through a bitter war, had been prisoners of war, and who had managed to escape by sheer chance. Life was precious for them, and they were not going to waste their time with someone who was boring. Life was to be shared with people who had a zest for it. They were not unkind—after all, they would spend time talking to a child as if that child truly mattered to them. But if an adult in their company bored them, they would initiate a game that would cause the boring soul to hastily leave the group without reluctance.

There were other awkward moments when I felt it was too hard to make sense of my family's odd behaviour. My mother hated to cook. She viewed it as a chore that required far too much work for very little reward. She did cook a great soup once a week, which we ate for the rest of the week. Any effort she put into cooking meant she wanted us to eat it all, as she created these dishes with her own two hands.

She had a saying she constantly used whenever my father asked for something from the kitchen. She would voice her protest. "Look," she would say. "I have only two hands and ten fingers. If God wished for me to serve another human being, then surely, He would have given me four hands and twenty fingers."

It was logic my father could not dispute. He made his own coffee.

The truth was my mother was a very busy person, and preparing meals seemed to be a great challenge for her. However, she was a wonderful baker, and she could whip up a treat in no time at all. She considered baking a creative work, and she did produce some masterful pieces. She was even able to make her own filo dough, something I witnessed two or three times. I watched her one day as she took the small ball of dough and stretched it over my father's conference table (which stood in our basement and it was there because there was no room for it in his office downtown). My mother stretched the dough and stretched it until it covered the whole table. Then she took her scissors and cut it into manageable squares. She loved apple strudel, which required the homemade filo dough in order to be worthy of eating.

When my friends came to visit, she might offer a sandwich, a slice of torte, homemade donuts, or some other treat. One evening, a friend came to see me, and we were having a quiet discussion on the back deck when my mother announced that the turkey was ready to eat. This was about ten o'clock at night. She called us into the kitchen and there it was—a majestic looking roasted bird. There was nothing else.

So, I said in Ukrainian, "Do we get something with this?" She looked perplexed. "How about a piece of bread?" I suggested. "Of course," she said. "That's a good idea. I just thought, here it is: a roasted turkey ... really, nothing comes close to a freshly roasted turkey, so I wanted you and your friend to have a taste."

We did have a taste. A slice of bread and a juicy slice of turkey breast. I knew that my mother felt she had done her job. She had provided us with some sustenance, and there would be turkey for the family to eat for two or three days.

A few years later, when I met my future husband, he used to visit every other week. He worked for a newspaper in Ottawa as a reporter. On his days off, he would drive down to Toronto to see me. Being in an unusually gracious mood, my mother said I should invite him for dinner.

Unfortunately, my mother had an issue to deal with, and soon forgot that we would be having a guest for dinner. Although Alan had been to the house a few times, she had never met him. Well, there was a flurry in the kitchen, and out came an assortment of dishes, which we ate. Then we had dessert. We always had some kind of sweet in the house in case someone dropped in. As we were eating our almond loaf (one of Mother's favourite desserts), she walked into the kitchen to make more tea. To her horror, she discovered that the mashed potatoes were still in the pot and had not been served. Her solution to this dilemma was to call us all back to the table as she served up portions of mashed potatoes. I explained to a bewildered Alan to simply eat the potatoes, as life would be much easier this way.

I asked her, "Why are you serving potatoes now?" Well, she pontificated on the amount of work needed to make mashed potatoes, and the least any of us could do is respect her effort and eat the bloody potatoes. It sort of made sense and it sort of didn't, but I could not justify why anyone would want to eat potatoes after a hefty slice of almond loaf.

I guess eccentric people did not scare him. He did marry me. He remembers the potato fiasco, but regards it as a charming idiosyncrasy characteristic of my mother.

People who knew her knew that there was another side to her. She had a big heart. She gave away lots of money, even when times were tough. She helped a lot of people, was very involved in community projects, and worked very hard to free Ukrainian women writers serving time in the Gulag in Siberia. I wish I had paid closer attention to her work—especially her involvement with the writers sentenced to hard labour camps for their writing, their embroidery, and their nationalistic feelings. Woman's World, the magazine she edited and put together for years, was a platform to expose the horrific reality facing Ukrainian intellectuals who had been left behind. More on this later.

Although she loved to have fun, she did present a serious and no-nonsense persona. As the stern principal of the Ukrainian school, I knew the naughty ones amused her. When she told us the stories about her trials as a principal, it was always with a twinkle in her eye and a smile on her face. She enjoyed them all. There was such a contrast between my serious mother and my fun-loving mother.

A family photo after a community event. We look prosperous and well.

Mrs. Max

Mrs. Max (my nickname for her) was a great friend of my mother's. She truly was a character. Her husband and my father had a longstanding friendship. I do not remember the Max family from Austria, but I have vague childhood recollections of visiting someone in a refugee camp. I understood it had been the Maxes. At the same time, we had been in a safe house in Austria. I do remember them very well from when we were all in the same house in Winnipeg. Eventually, we all migrated to Toronto.

Mrs. Max was a great cook, and she often whipped up food for us which we all enjoyed. Mrs. Max was not only a great cook; she was also a wonderful storyteller. In Toronto, the Maxes had a kitchen and a living room/dining room combination. There was a sofa on which we would sit and listen to her stories. My sister and I would wander there after dinner to be entertained by Mrs. Max's storytelling. Her repertoire was amazing—a never-ending list of stories she could dish out for us children.

What I did not know then was that children were not her only audience. Ukrainian visitors to Toronto knew about Mrs. Max's reputation as a storyteller and would often request a session. These sessions were held late at night, when all the children were asleep, when Mrs. Max would entertain an audience with stories that were for adult ears only. She was often referred to as a storyteller who was as compelling as the storyteller Scheherazade from "One Thousand and One Nights."

Mrs. Max was extremely generous. If you entered her home, there was always a treat for you. We loved to go there. It was a busy and exciting home, and it was full of laughter and fun.

I loved Mrs. Max. Later in life, when she was widowed, she had a tiny apartment on Bloor Street opposite High Park. If I came home for Christmas in January, my sister and I would pay her a visit. Usually, her daughter would be there, visiting from Montreal.

One Christmas, we wandered over to Mrs. Max's apartment to pay our respects. Her daughter opened the door as Mrs. Max called out, "Who is it?" When she saw us, she ordered her daughter to "get out the Dubonnet—we have special visitors!" She was so pleased to see us, and we were delighted to be entertained by her for an hour or so.

My sister told me a story about Mrs. Max a few years ago. At that time, I had a sessional job at the University of Prince Edward Island giving a course on how to teach English to newcomers to Canada. I liked to tell this story to my students, but I had to choose my audience for it carefully. I did not wish to insult anyone who couldn't handle a swear word or two.

At eighty-five, Mrs. Max had decided she needed to drink decaffeinated coffee. She called up her son and told him to help her master the phrase "decaffeinated coffee" in English. He taught her, and they practised until Mrs. Max felt she was ready to walk up the hill to the No Frills store and look for her decaffeinated coffee.

Up the hill she went. It was about 3:30 in the afternoon and the kids were going home from high school. Some of the boys were on bicycles and were busy amusing themselves with vulgar words that were taboo in school and more than likely not allowed at home either. As they tore down Bloor Street, they were yelling "fuck you" back and forth at each other.

By the time Mrs. Max entered the No Frills store, she was still muttering the new word for decaffeinated coffee in English—at least, her version of it. She wandered over to the coffee shelf and searched for her new brand. She had no luck.

She was well known to the staff as she was a regular visitor to the store. So she wandered over to the cash register and said, "Please, help. I need defuckanated coffee." Well, the place erupted with laughter, but they knew what she wanted and got it for her. Home she went, embarrassed and upset with her son. "You did it deliberately, didn't you?!" she accused him.

His protests were to no avail, but he did figure it out, and explained to his mama that those nasty young punks were really responsible for her mistake. All was forgiven. I never knew her to hold a grudge.

As much as I liked Mrs. Max, you were not permitted to ignore her requests. At twelve years of age, I made such a mistake. She called my house to say her daughter should come home. I ignored the request for a good hour before I told her daughter she was wanted at home. I paid for that dearly.

Not long after the call, I popped in to visit the Max family and was told in no uncertain terms to leave. I was so humiliated, but I learned a lesson. When an adult makes a reasonable request, you have to honour it. I never told my parents about it, and I do not think Mrs. Max did either, because it was never spoken of again.

I know she did not hold a grudge, as she quite often told me nice stories about myself later on. She particularly liked to tell me that as a child, I had been very generous. I received a chocolate bar from someone, possibly a family friend. A real prize—a whole chocolate bar for me. Apparently, I took it to Mrs. Max and asked her to cut it into small pieces so I could share it with the other children in the house. She commented on that gesture quite a few times. I'm not so sure it had been generosity on my part. I wasn't quite sure how I could eat it all by myself with other children in the house. Only at Christmas, when every child received a whole chocolate bar, could you eat one all by yourself.

Other Accomplishments

While I was in high school, my mother decided to obtain a Master's Degree in Slavic Studies. A small group of Ukrainians, all working toward obtaining the same degree, would travel every second week to the University of Ottawa to do the coursework.

The University of Ottawa accepted credits from Eastern European universities. My mother was overjoyed to be accepted into the program. She had obtained her undergraduate degree from the university in the beautiful Polish city of Krakow. Her Polish was excellent, too—and everyone who applied to the program needed to speak and write in two Slavic languages. Most had three.

There were ten students who travelled to Ottawa in two big cars. They would leave Friday afternoon and come back late Saturday night. They did this for two full years. Regardless of the long travel time, my mother loved being back in school. Fluent in Polish and Ukrainian, she also had a good understanding of Russian. My mother's ability with languages was innate. She loved to write and read mostly in Ukrainian, but there were a few books in other languages scattered around our house. During her Slavic studies, she would discuss the reading assignments in whatever language they were written.

The small group of adults studying for their Master's were an interesting collection of mostly Ukrainian writers. Among them was Borys Oleksandriv Hrybinsky, a Ukrainian poet, who would make up poetry that would make them all laugh. He was a respected and well-known poet, and a lovely, gracious person who spoke eloquently to everyone, even us youngsters. My mother would quote his car travel poetry, and his ability to create it on the spot made an impression on me.

Borys Oleksandriv Hrybinsky arrived in Canada in 1949. He was a recognised and well-known young poet. His first book of poetry, Moyi Dni ("My Days"), was published in 1946 in Salzburg, Austria. Poetry was his preferred genre, but he also wrote articles and critiques that appeared in Ukrainian newspapers. He was a known humorist and a satirist, and when writing in these two styles, he used the pseudonym "Svyryd Lomachka." He had an interest in and was a translator of French Quebecois poetry. Another of his achievements was establishing the Canadian branch of the Union of Ukrainian Writers called Slovo ("Word"). He was the head of this organisation. He was well liked, respected, and admired not only by fellow writers, but by everyone in our community.

Years later, in 1979, he was killed on Christmas Eve by a drunk driver. The community mourned him, and my parents were shattered by the event.

* * *

When my mother was away in Ottawa, my father was in charge of us. She always left baked goods. He was a terrible cook and had no idea what to put on the table. I have no recollection of him giving us anything hot and nutritious. Eggs were what my parents often relied on. That finally came to an end when my sister developed a rash—an allergic reaction to the number of eggs we were consuming.

All of the Toronto adult students graduated and one, Nadia Popil, my mother's good friend, went on to be the department head of German and Slavic Studies at the University of Regina. She wanted my mother to join the faculty, but mother was ensconced in Toronto life, and there we stayed.

We drove to my mother's graduation—an incredibly boring affair. It put me off graduation ceremonies, so I never attended mine. Years later, I did attend two of my children's graduations, and actually enjoyed them.

My mother's degree from the University of Ottawa probably helped her become the principal of the Ukrainian high school. The classes were held in the newly constructed building, right next to St. Nicholas Ukrainian Greek Catholic Church on the corner of Queen Street and Bellwoods Avenue. It is a pleasant building with large sunny classrooms. Creative arts were usually taught by Myron Levytsky. Eventually, he began looking for someone to take his place. I had finished my university studies and found myself teaching

Ukrainian creative arts to the first-year students. Levytsky talked me into teaching the course.

"But I'm not qualified to teach creative arts! I don't even know where to begin."

He looked at me and shook his head. "It will be easy. I will prepare all your notes, and all you will have to do is write them out on the board. Have the students copy them."

So, that is what I did. Not a very inspiring way to engage students, but I guess it was better than hearing someone go on and on in a monotonous voice. This cheered me up, as I remembered my religion classes as incredibly boring. So the students wrote down my notes, and the time passed. I only did this for one year. One year was enough. But I will say I wish I had all those notes Levytsky wrote for me. They were interesting, colourful, and they gave students a good orientation on Ukrainian creative arts. He had a good sense of what was useful to know and what would be of interest to young students.

There was also a student choir at the high school. At the age of eighteen, my sister was the choral director. It was my mother's inspiration to have a young girls' choir sing and appreciate Ukrainian music. My sister was a University of Toronto music student who focused on choral directing and arranging harmonies. At a very young age, she nurtured a love for our wonderful music in all who heard it.

Kvitka started the choir Vesnivka at the school, and it has existed for over fifty years. It has travelled throughout the world bringing music to urban and rural areas, wherever there was a Ukrainian diaspora—in France, Italy, Poland, Portugal, and Argentina—and Ukraine. Under Kvitka's direction, the choir has won many awards and sang with prestigious choirs in Canada. Music is a universal language. As the choir grew in reputation, Ukrainian music gained greater appreciation and recognition within the Canadian and international music scene.

* * *

The serious side of my mother was evidenced by her commitment to Ukrainian community organisations. She enjoyed being a member and leading director of Plast, the Ukrainian Scout Movement. Her administrative work in Plast took up many hours, but she enjoyed it and very often came as camp director to Grafton, where the Ukrainian Scouts had bought a farm bordering Lake Ontario. While we slept in tents, her tent always had a cot on which she placed a sleeping bag. There were lots of jokes about our illustrious leader sleeping on a cot while the rest of us were in our sleeping bags on the ground. As far as I remember, no one resented that she used a cot. She was older, and with age came certain privileges.

She was sensible as camp leader: the focus was on learning life skills and on appreciating and emulating the scouting values, such as integrity and respect, as upheld in Ukraine and elsewhere in the world. We all enjoyed learning basic survival skills such as outdoor cooking, keeping fit, and pitching a tent. Our training sessions took us through wooded areas, where we found and read directions as to where to go next. We sent and received semaphore flag messages, and had to get from A to B in a certain timeframe. As we got older, the routes became more difficult and were a challenge to complete. But we loved these training sessions and considered them a game.

There was an emphasis at camp on sports. We practised and competed in Olympic sports. The usual ones were discus and javelin, speed running, high jumping, and so on.

There was also a Scouting obligation to learn a traditional craft practised in Ukraine. My group actually made a simple press modelled after the first printing press and displayed its ability to print leaflets. Another time, we chose a region in Ukraine and recreated that region's traditional art. I embroidered a blouse using a pattern typical of that area. It was time-consuming work, but in the end, I had something valuable to display. There were groups who chose other projects in order to gain another badge to sew onto their scout's shirtsleeve. These were small, round embroidered badges depicting the skills. I loved all the symbols of my accomplishments, and I had a number of them.

No doubt my mother was instrumental in developing the Scouting program, ensuring that whatever we undertook would be of interest to us. She loved her work in the Ukrainian Scout Organisation and worked alongside people like Tsiopa Paliiv, who, together with her very good friend Tonia Horokhovych, were involved in establishing the Women's Scout Movement in Ukraine. I knew both and was very impressed by their knowledge, their logic, and their commitment to their communities in Canada and in the homeland.

Tonia was frequently in our home. I knew her as a stellar scout and a gentle, kind person. I was told, and this impressed me, that this quiet person had the fortitude to play an active, dangerous and important role as a liaison between Ukrainian dissidents and the diaspora in the West.

There were many others, all very likeable and enthusiastic scouts, who involved Ukrainian children in enjoying, participating in, and respecting the values of the scouting movement. It was huge. Thousands of Ukrainian children in Canada and the United States were members.

Every few years, we hosted Ukrainian scouts from different parts of Canada and the United States, or we were invited and were hosted in different places. These jamborees were wonderful. They were a chance to show off the skills we had learned and the sports we excelled in. Competition was encouraged but expected to be undertaken in a good-natured way. The scout movement was a way to develop decent values and have respect for all humanity. It taught me a lot.

And yes, we knew how to march as a unit in our uniforms, our berets on our heads, always with a song to keep to the tempo and to shorten the time on long marches. We did them with pleasure, and we did them well.

My mother and Mrs. Pavlyshyn, the Scout camp's nurse.

Chaos, Fun, Determination

My mother's name is not easy to pronounce. That ya at the beginning of her name is a tricky sound. It's a very soft ya that sounds a lot like the end of the word papaya. Her name is Yaroslava. But as her daughter, I called her "Mamo," the vocative declension of Mama. That is why my three young children, imitating me, referred to her this way. To this day, that is what she is called. She did not seem to mind.

My father, realising that the grandchildren were imitating me, pulled me aside and said, "Do not refer to me as 'Tato,'" ("Father") "I do not wish to be called that." I called him "Dido" ("Grandfather"), and my children did, too. He was pleased with that.

Friends in Charlottetown who knew my mother, also referred to her as Mamo or Mrs. Z. But Mamo seemed easier—sort of catchy—and it stuck. Most of my friends enjoyed my mother. She was a good storyteller. Though her English was heavily accented, she spoke very well. Her sharp tongue was as effective in English as in Ukrainian.

She used to come for summer visits to PEI. She loved the water and could spend hours near the beach. My friend Rose Ellen often invited us to spend time at her cottage in Brudenell. It is a lovely spot. The cottage is large—four bedrooms—and it stands in a large field. The land slopes down to a sandy spit, which forms a shallow bay on the west side. Perfect for a woman who couldn't swim! We would deck her out with styrofoam noodles, and off she would go for her swim. At first, I had to go with her, but as she became more and more familiar with the shore, she gained confidence. The styrofoam noodles allowed her to float effortlessly and fearlessly.

We were able to buy a shore lot from Rose Ellen's sister, where we built a small, rustic cottage, which my mother loved. She would visit for two to three weeks, and was a demanding guest. But that was OK with me. Breakfast had to be at eight o'clock sharp. On her holidays, she loved a big breakfast of eggs, bacon, toast, fruit, and coffee. This was a breakfast that suited her. Having finished her morning meal, she would be ready to begin the day at the shore.

I would watch with amusement as she packed up for her outing. First there were the hats—three of them on her head, one on top of the other. When I questioned why she would need three hats, she explained the first one was to keep her hair out of the way, the next was to secure and hold down the first, and the third was to protect her face from the sun. In addition to the hats and the styrofoam noodles, she organised and packed her reading material—books, newspapers, her glasses, her notebook and pencil—all packed into a flight bag marked "Astro," a Ukrainian travel company, whose owners were her friends. Equipped with her swimming noodles and her bag of reading materials, she made her way down to the shore.

Anyone watching my mother making her way to the water would be entertained by the three hats and the different styrofoam noodles around her. She was a sight, but she didn't care - this was her holiday, and she was going to enjoy herself in her own way.

My husband, Alan, found a bench the water had carried to our beach—a solid bench we thought must have fallen into the water during a storm and gotten swept over onto our shore. It was a grand bench, long and wide. We pulled it up and placed it safely in a small, shaded area just a few steps from the beach. Alan bought my mother a nice piece of foam to cover the seat, and that made it a wonderful little hideaway. Down she would go after breakfast and sort herself out with her reading materials. She read, swam, and napped on the bench. Our little Scottie dog would walk down beside her and keep her company, in his favourite spot under the bench.

My mother was not fond of having animals in the house, but she liked Chibi (named by my daughter who, arriving home from Japan, took one look at the dog and named him "little one" in Japanese). My mother liked Chibi's perky ears, so she called the dog "Vushka" ("little ears"). She used to say, "That dog looks very intelligent—all he needs is a pair of glasses, and he'll be able to read my newspapers."

She would swim and read all morning, until I called her to come up to the cottage for lunch. I made big lunches, bigger than our dinners because this was the arrangement to which she was accustomed. She would come up to the cottage and announce, "Now, you know that I have a very delicate disposition. Don't give me too much." She would be offered a delicate portion, and when she finished that, she would often request one or even two more delicate portions. I was amused by her delicate disposition.

The only problem we had was that she liked to go to bed early. She wanted us to be quiet, and was definitely unhappy if someone dropped by in the evening. She would call out, "Tell them to go home! It's night, what are they doing out?" Thank goodness these pronouncements were in Ukrainian, so no one understood her. My friends would be concerned by her tone of voice. They thought perhaps she was in pain and needed something. Luckily, not too many came to the cottage at night, as I encouraged folks to consider daytime visits. Lunch was the way to go: a grand lunch would always put my mother in a good mood. She could be funny and rather sarcastic, she enjoyed the food—and, most of the time, the company.

Alan's cousin Maime came a few times to visit. She was a welcome guest, as she would spend time teaching mother how to float. Maime had a lot of patience, and eventually my mother could float for a short period. My mother was pleased, as was Maime. That summer, when my mother was leaving the Island, Maime arrived at the airport with a small jar of homemade jelly. "That's for learning how to float. Next year, there will be a bigger present, because you will learn the breaststroke." My mother was very fond of Maime, and flashed her one of her best smiles. She called her Mariianka—a diminutive of Mary Ann. Maime liked it.

One of my mother's favourite hobbies was to forage in the woods for mushrooms. She picked about six to seven different varieties in Ontario. I did pick them with her on occasion, but I was usually part of the mushroom processing team. Picking mushrooms with my mother was a ritual of almost religious proportion. She knew her mushrooms, and we picked only the ones she was absolutely positive were not poisonous. I learned a lot about what to pick and what not to touch. She liked to dry, pickle, or marinate the mushrooms. These were put away in jars to have when the cold wind and the snow made life difficult, but we also had them fresh in a variety of dishes. The smell and taste of those delicate dishes are still part of my childhood memories.

In Ontario, we had a cottage in the Muskoka region. There were three cottages that belonged to Ukrainians, and three women who competed seriously to collect the greatest amount of mushrooms.

It would be early morning, just as the sun was coming over the horizon, when the mushroom-picking frenzy would begin. My mother would put on her mushroom-picking outfit—a warm top, baggy pants, good solid shoes to tramp through the woods, always a hat, a basket, and a large walking stick. The stick was very important. It had two uses: one was to turn over the leaves to hunt for mushrooms hiding under the foliage, and the other was to scare off any animals that might threaten her.

She would sneak out quietly into the backwoods and pick to her heart's content. There were many varieties, and she would be back before breakfast to show off her haul. I learned which mushrooms were the best and which were deadly. If I didn't recognise it, I didn't touch it.

When she ventured out for mushrooms, she would pick enough to cover a picnic table. No matter what we picked, mother examined them all. The cepes (boletus edulis) were better than gold. She would exclaim in wonder as she caressed them gently. Here was a symbol of the wonderful smell of a homeland forest in the Carpathian mountains and of all the splendid mushrooms that grew there. For her, the cepes were mushroom royalty; they represented all that was wonderful in life.

She would lay all the mushrooms out on the picnic table so that the sun warmed them up and encouraged any bugs to move out. After the sunbathing, we cleaned the lovely fungi, washed them gently, and prepared them for a variety of treatments. This was time-consuming work.

Back in PEI, when she first came to Rose Ellen's cottage, after she was settled, we would head out for a walk. I took her to the back of the property, where I knew little yellow treasures were popping up from the ground. There they were—a plethora of dainty-looking chanterelles. What a grand surprise! I told her what they were called in English. She immediately renamed them "Cinderellas." To her, they looked like swirling gowns, like the one Cinderella wore to the ball. If you look at a cluster of chanterelles, they do look like they are dancing. Their tops are like skirts, curled under at the edges and leaning slightly over, giving the impression of movement. They are lovely to look at, and their brilliant yellow colour is a cheerful sign of beauty and a promise of gourmet delight.

She was excited to find we had mushrooms on the Island. Both Rose Ellen's cottage and our own, right next door, are situated on soil that encourages chanterelles to grow. They are plentiful—especially after a rainfall. One of my daughters, who lived in Montreal at that time said, "You know. Mum, you could pay for Mamo's flight if you just came to Montreal with a suitcase full of chanterelles. People pay over fifty dollars for a pound." It was a tempting idea, but it just wasn't going to happen. As it was, we ate plenty of mushrooms and gave many away to friends. I occasionally picked and cleaned a bunch of chanterelles and placed them in a nice, small bag and gave them out as hostess or birthday gifts. Another one of my mother's bright ideas. "Take the Cinderellas—nothing compares to that kind of gift!"

Mushroom frenzy near Huntsville—my mother knew her mushrooms and loved to pick them.

We stayed in Charlottetown when the weather was cool or when some cottage construction work needed to be done. Our house had a huge front porch. When we bought the house, the porch was glassed in and divided into two sections. At first, we took down the section that had the only door to the street: one had to go through that door in order to come into or out of the house.

The other section of the porch, on the left, stayed glassed in for a few more years. It had its own entrance and exit doors. It was a good place to put up a visitor. The doors had screens and locks and provided a suitable place for pleasant naps on the couch. It was cool, quiet and the porch couch was popular. Besides the couch, there was a pine box that could serve as a coffee table, and there was a night table upon which stood a good reading light. Finally, there were Roman shades on the windows, providing total privacy.

When someone asked my mother how she was getting along, she indicated she was well. Then, if the person asked, "And how is your accommodation?" My mother's tongue-in-cheek reply was, "Very nice, yes, almost outside."

When we were in town, she and the Astro bag of reading materials would walk down to the boardwalk. Most of the time, she would stay for a couple of hours reading and watching the water and the people parading along the boardwalk. She had picked out the best bench on the boardwalk as her own—it looked out at the opening of the harbour and provided the sitter with all the activities playing out on the water. Every once in a while, she came home disgruntled. I would ask, "What's the matter?" She would make a face (an actor and writer by profession, her facial expressions were legendary) and say, "Someone is sitting on my bench!", to which I would say, "Listen, it's a public boardwalk—you don't own the bench." That wouldn't please her, but she would settle down on the porch with her reading materials and be partially pacified.

The one thing she did not like about being in town was the fact we had a lot of company. It was too noisy, and people stayed too late: why did I not do anything about this? Then, one evening, I heard her say, "Mr. Rice, you want cake?" Well, Mr. Rice thought he would like some cake. "Yes. That would be lovely." She cut him a piece of cake and said, "Good, you eat cake, you go home." Mr. Rice was not impressed. I'm sure he thought this woman was very rude. On the other hand, she did the same thing to Maime, saying, "Mariianka, you want cake?" Followed by, "Good, you eat cake, you go home," Maime laughed. "I understand that. She wants to go to bed. What the hell, so do I." She ate her cake and more than likely got a piece to take home because she respected my mother's wishes. And besides, she was a favourite.

But her very favourite person in Charlottetown and on the whole Island was Heather Orford, one of my oldest friends. She loved Heather and her sister Nancy, but Heather was the absolute, unequivocal favourite. One day, when I phoned my mother, I could tell she was entertaining. She told me her visitors were writers from Kyiv. Such interesting women and so very charming. "Almost as charming as your friend Heather," she said.

Heather deserved the praise. She lived two doors down from us, and would keep an eye out for my mother. She was very kind to her. She took my mother for little walks in the square in front of our houses. When my mother would get "sideways in her box," an expression of grumpiness that I think was used by Clifford, Heather's dad, she was there to listen. Heather could read my mother as she sat on a bench in our park. Her body language said it all. At times, I disappointed my mother, but Heather knew how to placate her, and would arrange lunches and coffees and storytelling. My mother would be on her best behaviour with Heather. She was very fond of her.

After my mother died in 2009, I spent quite a few weeks dealing with her estate. Heather flew down to help clean up and sort out the apartment. But she ended up painting the apartment instead, because the sorting needed my sister's input, which she couldn't give at the time. I don't know too many people who would spend that kind of money to fly to Toronto to help a friend. Death in the family can be very taxing for everyone involved, but that sort of kindness does make a difference. I was grateful she came. Heather stayed with me in my mother's apartment and I had someone to talk to and share my memories of my mother, an inspiring soul.

* * *

I miss my mother. I miss our chats, and I realise I am losing my Ukrainian. Words are missing for me when I speak it. We would speak once or twice a week. She was a busy woman right to the day she had her stroke. When I called her, I often heard voices in the background. She would be hosting a meeting or having a conversation with a friend. She rarely talked about frivolous things. She would say, "There is so much to do." She was involved with many organisations, all working toward good causes. But one of her favourite causes was the book publishing business in Kyiv. It provided a venue for Ukrainian writers to publish and distribute their works. Quite a few of these books would be brought into Canada, mainly by Canadians travelling to and from Kyiv. I know she was instrumental in arranging these shipments, and I have no doubt she would bully people into supporting the company and the writers. The writers definitely needed an outlet for their work, and in her, they found a champion.

I flew to Ukraine in 2007 on business for Holland College, PEI's post-secondary community college. At that time, the college was exploring possibilities of establishing educational programs in countries that might be interested in a partnership with a Canadian college. I was not alone—there were two others with me. We carried supplies for the schools we visited. We were introducing a more participatory and interactive teaching approach in education. This methodology challenged the more traditional, teacher-centred way of delivering knowledge. Holland College had a variety of similar programs running in China. I had been there three times, but now, the college was interested in other countries.

If we were going to Ukraine, I felt my colleagues needed to see Kyiv, the city where, in the year 1200, four hundred golden domed churches had stood on the hills. I also wanted them to see the UNESCO heritage church, St. Sophia, which had a remarkable interior, full of mosaics and frescoes.

The Olzhych Foundation is a publishing house located in Kyiv. My mother gave a lot of time and energy to this publishing house because it was another important cause for her. My mother was a staunch supporter and a keen fundraiser for the foundation. Her efforts did not go unnoticed. After her death, the Canadian branch of the Fundatsia Olzhych raised enough money to provide a scholarship in her name for a Ukrainian student studying journalism in Ukraine.

Oleh Olzhych was born on July 8, 1907. He was both a Ukrainian poet, and an archaeologist by profession. His poetry concentrated on Ukraine's struggle for independence. His work was widely read and influential. He was a member of the Organisation of Ukrainian Nationalists, and was a recognised national leader. In 1944, he was arrested by the Gestapo for his nationalistic activities. He was interred in Sachsenhausen Concentration Camp, where he was executed.

My mother considered him hugely important and influential. She saw him as an inspirational figure—a natural leader who died far too young, and whose death was a great loss to Ukraine. Because of her work with the Olzhych Foundation in Canada, she knew the staff, made a phone call, and arranged our stay in Kyiv.

Before I left, my mother gave me contacts for individuals connected to the publishing foundation who would look after us during our stay in Kyiv. She also gave me an order: "You will bring back a box of books." I had no idea how big the box was and how I was going to carry it and my luggage. I knew there was no way I could ignore the request, though. In my mind was a saying she used when she disciplined us: "What I say is sviate!" (sacrosanct). "You understand?! It is absolutely sacred!!" To say she was dramatic would be an understatement. Somehow, I had to get the books back to Canada. The books arrived for me to take, and to my relief, they were packed up and addressed to my mother. The publishing company provided a driver to take us to the airport, and he took my books and arranged for them to be part of my luggage. The books flew with me to Canada and were delivered to her apartment. An obligation fulfilled, no extra effort required—and no thanks provided.

After my mother's death, someone arrived from the University of Toronto's Slavic Department and looked through her library. She had a collection of first editions of some rare and valuable books. These went to the Slavic Department. As for the books from Kyiv, some of which I recognised, they went to a Ukrainian library so that they would be available for the public.

* * *

I have two stories about my mother—one that underlines her status in the community and one which demonstrates her ability to laugh at herself.

My mother had many friends, a few of whom were very close. My sister's choir used to hold a fundraiser by organising a fashion show once a year. My mother attended, and usually picked two or three friends to go with her. My sister thought I should come and see the fashion show, as it would be a lot of fun and the fifty dollars included a very nice lunch with wine.

I arranged for Aline, a family member, to come with me. The two of us drove to Toronto from Ottawa. My mother was pleased to see us and quickly announced that we would need to take both my car and hers, as her friends were arriving at the house to be driven to the fashion show. She had reserved a table for eight. That meant there were seven friends to be chauffeured in two cars. Aline, who is married to Alan's cousin Jimmy, would drive my car, and I would drive my mother's.

I asked my mother why her friends would want to be bothered to come by bus to her house instead of staying on the bus till they reached the place where the show would take place. Well, she felt it was a very long bus ride, and really, it would be nice if they could just come by car and go home by car.

Aline and I were not expecting to be a taxi service but what did it matter? We had nothing else on our agenda. Mother organised her friends. Everyone settled in, and away we went.

Now, a woman I really liked, who was a good storyteller, was in our car. I was listening to her, not paying attention to my mother, who was busy telling me to drive in this lane or that, or to pick up speed, as she was convinced we would be late. Every few seconds, she had a comment about my driving, but I paid no attention. She was a terrible driver, but had no trouble telling everyone else how to drive. She got annoyed with me. "You are not doing what I think you should be doing." And then she turned around and said to her friend. "Be quiet, she is too busy listening to you to pay attention to me."

I was horrified. I could not believe the order, or the tone in which she spoke to her friend. We arrived at the venue and mother hurried ahead, presumably to make sure they had been given a good table. In the meantime, I fell into step with Stefa, my mother's friend who had just received a tongue-lashing. I asked her why she allowed my mother to talk to her in such a harsh manner. She just smiled and said, ""Well, my dear," (in Ukrainian, "my golden one") "your mother has such an artistic temperament. It's OK—really, it is."

The other story occurred on a Sunday. Every Sunday morning, my mother drove to church in her very well-cared-for car. One Sunday, she picked up her friend Tonia and turned left onto Queen Elizabeth Drive. She realised that it was late and stepped on the gas. It didn't take long for a police siren to signal for her to stop. A young policeman walked up to the car and asked my mother for her licence. Tonia was irritated by the delay and said in Ukrainian, "What does that idiot want from you?" A few minutes later, the officer leaned toward my mother and said, in perfect Ukrainian, "This idiot is only charging you half of what he should be charging you." The two women thought the whole thing was very funny and chuckled all the way to church.

* * *

My mother loved all her grandchildren. Kvitka was her first grandchild. My father and mother drove to PEI to see this wonder child. They didn't come alone—Olha Zelena (the green lady's daughter), who was a high school teacher and a very close friend of the family, came along. Besides being good company, she helped with the driving. Quite unexpectedly, Mrs. B called and asked if she could come, as she had never travelled very much in Canada and very much wanted to see Atlantic Canada and the ocean.

They arrived and stayed for ten days. The three women were great with the baby. Kvitka was a busy, busy baby. She could stay up until almost 11 p.m. and be up again at 5 a.m. I was exhausted, but there were three souls ready to entertain her as soon as she woke up. They took her to the beach, doted on her, and photographed her constantly. My mother had a small slide viewer which held her favourite picture of her grandchild in it. Only the one picture was kept there. She could look at Kvitka's picture all the way home, and she joked that anyone who wished to have a look would be charged twenty-five cents for the privilege.

She loved my story of our first boat crossing with the baby to the mainland. I was in the bathroom changing the baby when a pleasant-looking older lady walked in. She looked at my child and said, "Oh, what a pretty baby. What do you call her?"

I hesitated. The Island did not have many immigrants, and my child had a very unusual name. I took a deep breath and said, "I call her Kvitka." The woman looked at me with a disapproving face and said, "Oh, I don't think she'll thank you for that when she grows up."

My parents were enjoying the visit. My father did not like the beach, but he loved napping and reading and being left alone in peace. One day, the rest of us had taken off for the beach. The house was quiet and he was having a good rest when he heard a car drive up. My in-laws had come to visit my parents. Alan happened to return to the house for something at one point and told me, "All I could hear was three adults yelling at each other." He called his dad out to the kitchen and said to him, "He's not deaf. You can yell, but he still won't understand."

When I finally arrived home, my father was out of sorts. He said, "What could I do? I couldn't communicate with them. I offered coffee, salami, cheese, bread, and cake. Preparing a snack gave me something to do, away from them, and something that would help pass a little time." I have no idea how he had managed to offer them anything, but I think he must have hauled the stuff out and arranged some sort of snack on a tray. They showed no interest in the food. He was out of his depth. I laughed. He was not amused.

I teased him: "You could have hidden upstairs and pretended to be asleep."

"I wasn't fast enough—they caught me looking out the window."

This was not the time to tell him a few English lessons would have helped. He never mastered English, and we never spoke it at home.

My three children were born on the Island. We moved to Ontario after they started school. Years later, Kvitka ended up as a teacher, living and working in Toronto. She visited her grandmother and did odd little jobs for her. They did things Mamo enjoyed. Kvitka drove her to the cemetery to visit Dido and fix up his grave. Kvitka drove her to the cottage, where there were always things to do.

My mother's cemetery visits and her advancing years started to worry her. Where would she be laid to rest? She had bought four plots at Prince Edward Cemetery, in her neighbourhood, and four more plots in the Ukrainian cemetery thirty kilometres outside of Toronto. She wanted to have a place for my father, herself, and two for her daughters in each location. We had to explain that we would not be buried beside her. This created a dilemma for her.

The plots in the Ukrainian cemetery were too far away. The neighbourhood cemetery's plots were stacked, two over two. My father had died a long time ago and he went into the bottom plot. She wanted to be beside him when it was her time. Now that our mother knew that my sister and I had other burial plans, she wanted to get the cemetery staff to lift up my father so she could be on the same level and not so far down in the ground.

I suggested to her she could go in the top plot, over him, and sell the other two plots. She was horrified. "What, you think we should sleep beside strangers?" The suggestion that perhaps if she was not willing to sell the plots she could give them away to someone who didn't have the resources to buy any plots fell on deaf ears. There was no way she would be sleeping next to someone unknown.

She got her way. She paid a bundle to have my father lifted to the top level. It was a major job, as he had been buried in a stone sarcophagus. Up he went, and when the time came, she would be buried beside him. She was happy.

As she got older, our phone conversations usually began with me saying. "How are you, Mamo?"

"Well, I'm very busy" was the answer.

"What are you doing? Why are you so busy?" I would ask.

"Well, I'm busy packing," she would reply.

"Where are you going?" I would ask.

"To the next world, of course" was the answer.

This meant she was organising her papers and her newspapers. The papers were everywhere. I spent almost every night for five weeks cutting out marked articles and putting them into different boxes destined for two Ukrainian organisations and a magazine. When I finished, I had three large boxes full to the top with articles she had collected with useful information for the recipient organisations.

The sad thing was that nobody wanted the articles, because they already had the originals on microfiche. I was angry and devastated. She had spent so much time collecting and keeping the articles as resources, and no one seemed interested. There were easier ways to collect information. Regardless, it was the only time I put my foot down and demanded they come and take their box away. I could not throw the boxes out. I just couldn't. They did come, and the boxes disappeared.

* * *

My mother pronounced my middle child anaemic. Larissa was very blond and very pale. She loved to paint, and my mother wanted her to come and spend her March break in Toronto. Off went Larissa, and my mother booked egg-decorating lessons for her with a woman who was an enthusiastic and professional Ukrainian egg decorator. My mother would drive Larissa to and from her lesson, where she learned how to apply the wax and colour the egg. In later years, she could produce some beautiful eggs.

A Ukrainian Easter egg is called a pysanka. Pysanky are time consuming to create because they are delicate and intricate. They are based on regional designs handed down from generation to generation. The most intricate pysanky come from the Carpathian Mountains, where the Hutsuls live. Their embroidery and pysanky are dazzling. Their work is ornate, detailed, and exquisite. Larissa produced a few pysanky in the style of that region when she was twelve. The design is there, but the execution is very childlike.

I have Larissa's first efforts in a glass bowl on the sideboard in the dining room. Today, with two young children, she doesn't have the time, energy, or space for egg-decorating. Perhaps when she retires, she'll go back to it. Both Kvitka and Larissa have steady hands. They know how to create a lovely pysanka and how to embroider bookmarks with traditional Ukrainian patterns.

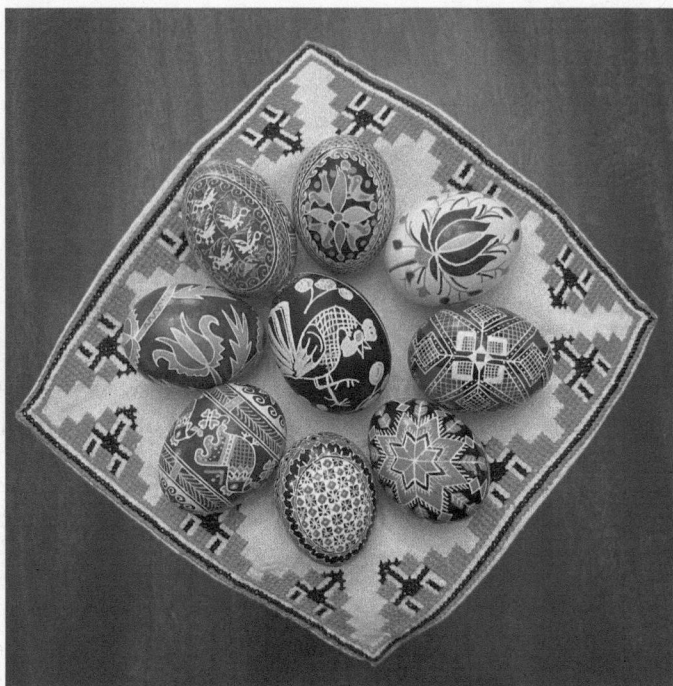

Pysanky from my collection, with patterns from various parts of Ukraine.
The middle egg, with a stylized rooster, was created by my daughter Larissa, and is based on a traditional design.

As for my youngest daughter, Zoja, my mother felt she was the most like her, in looks, spirit, and character. Mamo saw herself in her. She once said to me, with great admiration, "That one, I'm telling you—no one, no one, spits in her soup." Zoja was lively and could get my mother to agree to anything.

She was allowed to clean her fridge (a very big deal), tidy her kitchen, and more. All because she taught my mother how to use the microwave.

My mother had poor eyesight, and all Zoja did was put a red marker around the express button. This was huge. Mamo worked that microwave as if she was working a complex machine.

When Zoja was born, my in-laws thought that she looked like Alan's brother John. I told my mother the Holmans were claiming Zoja as their own.

"What do they know?"

I don't actually think she looks like my mother, but she sure has her tongue. She's very capable with her quick, witty, sarcastic retorts.

My sister has two daughters, both pretty and talented. However, as I have always lived far away, I have never spent much time with them. I cannot do them justice nor can I tell you about their relationship with their grandmother. But I do know that my mother considered all five of her granddaughters to be special, talented, and beautiful. She loved them all unconditionally.

When my mother's sister Zenia died in 1994, my mother and I went back to Ukraine to deal with her estate. This trip was very difficult for my mother. She had supported her sister throughout the years, hoping her life would be comfortable. It became obvious things had not been easy for my aunt. She lived in a tiny, miserable apartment, and my aunt gave up her bedroom to a young mother and her two school-age boys. She slept on the sofa in the living room.

Zenia allowed the family to live with her because the boys' mother worked in Lviv and she wanted her boys to go to a city school. How they all lived in that small space is bewildering to me, but it was very common in Ukraine. The young mother came from a family my aunt knew. She was from the village next to the one my aunt grew up in. The young mother's father was the village priest. Both my aunt and my mother knew the family and had a high regard for the parents.

While my mother and I were there, the young boys were in the village visiting their grandparents. We went to visit them, and our time there was very pleasant. The village was lovely. What surprised me was how freely the chickens, ducks, and other creatures roamed throughout the village. I wondered how the villagers knew which birds were theirs and which weren't. The mystery was settled for me when, in the evening, the owners came out and all had a special call. Chickens, ducks, and geese came running to their own barns to settle down for the night. It was quite the sight.

That evening, we returned to Lviv. There seemed no reason not to let the young mother and her two sons stay in the apartment. She seemed a decent sort, and her two boys were polite and well mannered. What harm could they do? The arrangement seemed to suit everyone involved.

It was only when we returned to Canada that we realised the young mother was determined to obtain ownership of the apartment. We gave her the apartment to use for as long as we didn't need it. It was free. No rent would be collected. We only asked her to agree to pay for the heat and gas, which, at the time, was very little. She didn't do that, because she knew the apartment would be taken away from us if the utilities were not paid, and if that happened, she could then apply to take it over. It's not quite clear to me why this was so.

My mother was furious. She had suspected the young woman's possible intentions. People were desperate to own property so that they could live in the city. It was hard to believe that when things didn't go as intended, the young mother vandalised the apartment.

There was some talk about saving the apartment for our family in Kazakhstan, who wanted to return home. In the end, we had to sell it, as the whole thing became too problematic for my mother. What was unknown to the young mother was the extent of our connections in Ukraine—friends who helped resolve this mess.

I felt sorry for her, but her deceitful behaviour alarmed me. She had seemed so pleasant. Her parents were gracious and decent people. They were not aware of their daughter's shocking behaviour. Her father wrote to my mother in Canada because he had a difficult time understanding what had caused the disagreement. He asked my mother to please write to him so he could mend the relationship. She did write him, but he was in his nineties, and she couldn't tell him about the vandalism, only that we needed the apartment for our family.

The young mother was foolish. The family in Kazakhstan never did return. She could have lived there till her boys were ready to move on.

My mother was nervous that everyone in the apartment complex knew we were from Canada. We were careful not to stand out. Regardless, we looked to be and were considered financially privileged people. The people who lived in these apartments, including my aunt, had been forced to give up their homes in exchange for very basic, small spaces. Most residents were friendly, but a few were bitter about their losses and circumstances.

My mother wanted to go through my aunt's things. She needed to do this quietly and behind closed curtains. Every night, my mother would pull the curtains shut, and we looked for things we had given my aunt over the years. We moved very quietly, so no one would know we were searching the place, the walls being very thin. We could see nothing of any value. However, under the sofa, we found all the stuff we had sent her so that she could sell it on the black market: leather gloves, sweaters, nylons and so on. All there, waiting for harder times before she would part with her treasures. My poor, unfortunate aunt had thought harder times were in her future.

A cupboard stood in the room. My mother knew that if her sister held on to the stuff we sent her, then somewhere in that room would be the money she had sent her. We searched the cupboard and took everything out of it, but there was no money. There was nowhere else to hide it. I looked at the cupboard and wondered if it came in two sections. I suggested that we try to lift off the top. It was heavy and it was awkward, but we lifted it off successfully. There, scattered, lay several hundred dollar bills. It was a shock to think my aunt deprived herself of basic necessities. We knew her life was hard, but the revelation that she hoarded the things that my mother sent her was disturbing.

We gave away the items under the sofa. The money, my mother doled out carefully to family members. It would not be much in Canada, but a thousand dollars in Ukraine was a fortune in 1994. It would be a lot even today.

* * *

While in Lviv, my mother decided on a trip to the Carpathian Mountains. We hired a driver who would take us to visit an artist whose work my mother admired, whom she wanted to meet. He lived in the foothills of the Carpathian Mountains, less than two hours' drive from Lviv. It was a great idea.

I was excited. I would get to see the mountain range and the villages along the way. The countryside and villages were dotted with small, efficient houses and huge gardens. People had land they worked, from which they harvested their crops and produced their winter supply of fruits and vegetables. The gardens were amazing, and everyone seemed to have a good understanding of how to get the most out of the soil. I was told that people planted their crops in a particularly organic way. Beets were planted alongside poppies—a beet, a poppy, a beet, a poppy and so on. It is a labour-intensive way to grow both beets and poppies. However, the crops looked very healthy. The other big crop was potatoes. Lots of potatoes were growing in all the gardens. We ate quite a few potatoes in Ukraine, and they were delicious—very different in taste from our potatoes here.

Beets create the base for borshch, beet soup. There are many variations of beet soups and dishes, all popular, and a dish or two are usually featured at every festive occasion. Poppyseeds are mostly used in baking. They make wonderful fillings in cakes and rolls. Baking a poppyseed torte is considered quite an achievement.

For me, the most exciting sight along the way to the foothills were the huge storks strutting along in their strange, awkward manner through the fields. I could watch them all day. They are considered the national bird of Ukraine and are cared for and cherished by the locals. Ukrainians love their storks—they are omens of good luck.

If the weather is too cold, people open up their barns and cover the floor with straw so the storks have a warm place to rest. If food is scarce, people feed the storks. Thousands of storks fly from Africa to Eastern Europe in the spring. These are large, majestic, white birds with black feathers at the tips of their huge wings. To see one up close is almost a spiritual experience.

As our car made its way through the small villages, I spotted a nest on the roof of a small one-storey house. The nest took up over a third of the roof, and I could clearly see a handsome stork standing up and surveying the view. I asked the driver to stop, and I pulled out my camera in hopes of getting a decent picture of the nest and the stork. I couldn't seem to angle the camera in a way that would capture what I wanted. Nothing for it but to climb onto the roof of the car and get my picture on more even footing.

I was holding my camera, thinking this would be a marvellous photo, when I spotted, out of the corner of my eye, a very distraught woman running toward me, holding a broom, with a look of real anger. She started to yell, "Leave our storks alone, you! You just leave the stork alone!" I realised she felt the stork was in danger, and I hollered back that I was just taking a znymka (not a word she understood). I should have said photografiia. By then, I could tell she was so enraged that I was definitely in trouble. I slid off the top of the car, hopped into it, and told the driver to get the hell out of there.

I do regret I upset her to the point that, had I not left, she would have broken her broom on me. She was that angry. Listening to my Ukrainian family members and their friends tell me how blessed one feels when storks set up residence in the neighbourhood, I realised I made a mistake. I should have made sure no one would misinterpret my intention.

The Funeral

In the Ukrainian tradition, eulogies are saved for the lunch or the dinner after the interment. Very little is said during the Mass. My mother's funeral was much grander than she ever wanted it to be. Her request for a very simple funeral with only family and about six of her closest friends was simply not to be. We had pressure from the community to honour her life with a celebration people could attend.

It was lavish and expensive, more like a wedding feast than a funeral dinner. People expected a grand occasion, even though they had to listen to far too many speeches. Mercifully, they were short. Some were colourful, and most were delivered by representatives of organisations to which my mother had given time and energy. None of the speeches stayed with me. The event remains a blur.

Our family friend Larysa Hwozdulych was the MC. For some reason, no one asked my own family if someone wanted to say a few words. There were just too many things to think about. It was a shock to see my husband negotiate a slot in the line-up with Larysa.

I had no idea what he would say. I did not think he would embarrass us, as he has always been very good on his feet. Mother's intellectual and sophisticated friends, her previous students, and certain dignitaries from different organisations made up most of the ninety people there. When Alan got up to speak, people looked intrigued by what this born-and-raised Canadian could possibly say about his very Ukrainian mother-in-law.

He went up to the podium with a glass of wine. My sister, very keen on the right optics, leaned over and said, "What is he doing?" I had no idea, and said so. We were all tense. As soon as he started, I knew it would be

OK. He was never lost for words, and as a journalist, he knew how to speak eloquently—most of the time.

He started off by comparing his Scottish background to our Ukrainian one. Two countries forever fighting for independence and freedom. He had that in common with Mamo and our community. It was a good introduction. Then, he proceeded to tell stories about his relationship with my mother.

She used to travel with us. She would fly to wherever we were and join us in our pop-up trailer, so it was the five of us, our dog, and sometimes our cat. When Alan worked for the CBC, he was asked to cover the premiers' conference in St. John's. Off we went in the van, pulling the trailer behind us. Alan had a very good friend there who had a lovely summer house in Brigus. Geoff Hiscock was a very generous man, and he insisted we use his summer home as a place to stay. The town was lovely and very picturesque. We loved it.

My mother arrived two days later. Alan met her at the airport and took her straight up to Signal Hill overlooking St. John's and the harbour. Mother was impressed. "Mamo, what do you think of this view?" he asked. Mamo looked like she was considering the question. "It's nice, it's very nice. It's not Venice, but it's nice." That was her assessment of the view. Alan always appreciated a good line. He loved what Mamo said, and he quoted her to quite a few politicians, who also enjoyed the line. Smart and snappy retorts were valued by Holman, my mother, and my three daughters, who very quickly realised a good line would get them out of any problem. They developed that skill at a fairly young age.

He brought my mother to Brigus, and she fell in love with the village. She supervised the girls' fishing activities, picked blueberries with them on the hill behind us, and walked through the little town, pointing out flora that interested her. She pointed out that hallucinogenic poppies grew in the ditches of that village. Geoff and his lovely wife Carla were taken with my mother and gave her a book featuring the flowers of Newfoundland.

Later on, in Toronto, I saw a small rock formation on her mantle and I asked her, "What is that?" She gave me a coy look and said, "That's my memory of Newfoundland. I took those rocks from the shore in Brigus and put them in my suitcase to bring home. Now, I have a little piece of Newfoundland right here, right in my living room."

In Newfoundland—my mother and my three children, Kvitka, Larissa, and Zoja.

Alan's second story was when Mamo joined us on our excursion to the West Coast. We picked her up in Edmonton and headed west. We toured Haida Gwaii (formerly the Queen Charlotte Islands) and Vancouver Island. Alan thought we should see Tofino, a renowned tourist town. The road to Tofino is twisted and very hilly. Alan was a fast driver, and my mother was nervous. This was a beautiful part of the country, only she could not enjoy it because we were going too fast. I felt her poke my back and say in Ukrainian, "If he wants to fly, then he should be a pilot—but we're on the ground, and he needs to slow down." I translated word for word, as there was no way to be diplomatic with the message. He slowed down.

He ended his tribute to his mother-in-law by saying, "Mamo was a respected Ukrainian, but she also was a very good Canadian! The Scots honour their dead with a toast. Would you please stand and toast Mamo's life?" They did. His talk appealed to the audience. They enjoyed the humour and the sentiment. It brought a certain closure to the tributes and the evening. I was pleased he did that for her—and for us. It was a fitting tribute from a son-in-law.

Back in Ukraine

In 2018, I returned to Ukraine with my husband. We walked through Mostyska and toured the town in which I'd been born. There aren't enough resources to rebuild and renew the town, and there is a downtrodden look about it: unfinished sidewalks, crumbling buildings, and one small square in the middle of town.

When I was there, the town held a celebration, which I attended with my cousins. A small band played live music, all kinds of food vendors were displaying their goods, and a jolly, spirited crowd were dancing their hearts out. Despite their poverty, their difficult lives, and their sad-looking town, they had the resolve to live as well as they could. It was a touching scene, and I realised I have had a very privileged life.

We had left Ukraine in 1944 and we were able to make it to Canada before the 1950s, a time when the Cold War was in full swing. My parents were desperate to find out what had happened to their families. When I was in Grade 3, my mother had been able to write to her family, but not directly. She did not use her own name on the envelope, instead styling herself as "Pani Kohut" ("Mrs. Rooster", a common name in Slavic countries). She needed to be absolutely certain no one would guess who was writing. The letters went first to an unknown but trusted source in Austria, then to contacts in Poland, and finally, to my grandparents in Ukraine.

She managed to correspond with her parents a few times. She was so happy to make that contact. It was all very involved and carefully executed. However, it did not last long—her mother died very soon after the letters arrived, and her father died a few years later.

It was devastating news for her. As a young child, I worried my mother would never recover from her grief. She cried for three days, and then pulled herself together. She had always hoped to see her parents again. It was not to be, but she did meet her younger sister in Budapest, years later.

Zenia, her youngest sister, had stayed behind to look after their parents. She was able to obtain a tourist visa to visit Budapest, and my mother flew to see her. My mother was going behind the Iron Curtain, and she was nervous. She spent a week with her sister, and I think it was a life-changing experience for her. After that visit, the mail kept coming and going at a steady pace. One could correspond more openly with family and friends after Stalin's death in 1953. My mother shipped packages twice a year to help her sister live better. I know she managed to buy her a small house in Lviv, which my aunt enjoyed for a short time.

When Nikita Khrushchev was elected First Secretary of the Communist Party of the USSR, he mowed down many houses, and up went the apartment buildings known as Khrushchevkas. My aunt was given a tiny apartment in a complex of four big apartment buildings. They were poorly built, ugly, and not well maintained.

When we were growing up, my mother's clandestine way of corresponding seemed absurd to us. However, when my sister and I met my father's family in 2016, we were shocked to find out my father's family had been hunted long after the war was over. There were six siblings—my father had one brother and four sisters. His brother had died early in life; however, three of the four sisters and their families were arrested and sentenced to hard labour camps in Siberia. The arrests occurred over four years, in 1947, 1949, and 1950. Two families received a sentence of seven years, except one family, who received a sentence of fifteen years. I met the eighty-two-year-old cousin, who had boarded the train for Siberia when she was ten and had not been released until she was twenty-five years old. Her childhood and her youth were lost to an unforgiving environment.

My father was eighteen years younger than his oldest sister. Her family was interrogated. Yevstakhiia, her daughter (my first cousin), told me she remembers the interrogation and how frightened she had been. She could not explain why they escaped the exile to Siberia.

The Gulag in Siberia was a terrible sentence. Each day, you were given one potato per person to eat and very little else. There were a few things one could do. In the summer, one could grow a garden and hope that what was harvested would help them survive the winter. To keep warm, families had to cut their own wood and keep the fire lit throughout the desperately cold nights.

The Gulag would have been our fate had we not escaped. What we did not know was that our extended family paid a heavy price because they could not reveal our whereabouts. The fact that they did not know made no difference, and their punishment was horrific: years of hard labour in a Siberian camp.

In 1994, my mother and I arrived in Lviv to settle my Aunt Zenia's estate. There, we met up with my father's cousin's family. My father and his cousin were close friends, and both had been in the Resistance. The cousin and his family were arrested on Christmas Eve 1949 and sentenced to seven years hard labour in Siberia. My father's cousin and his family survived the seven-year sentence and returned to Lviv, where they reestablished their former (pre-war) friendship with my mother's sister, Zenia. However, they were not able to tell us anything about our father's family in Mostyska. It seemed strange they knew nothing about who had survived and who hadn't. Perhaps they knew but would not tell. I asked someone about this and was told silence was normal, safer. No one wanted to be questioned about someone's fate. In 1994, people were still nervous about being interrogated. One does not forget that easily.

What surprised me about these cousins was their sense of humour. They were a jolly bunch, who joked about the pitiful compensation they received for their time in Siberia. What a contrast with their present life, when they could use any type of transport in Lviv for free. I was taken aback by their spirited nature, as a ticket for any city transport in 1994 cost less than one Canadian penny.

They took us out to the cemetery to visit Zenia's grave. She was beside her husband and her child, who had died at fifteen years of age. A hard and sad life, my aunt had. I was comforted to know she had a fairly large and extended family, and friends who liked and looked after her.

It is remarkable how we were able to reconnect with my father's family. Like my father, his family was musical and loved to listen and sing music. My father's sister's great-grandson had been visiting Lviv and, as was his habit, he popped into the music shop in search of a CD. He found a Canadian Ukrainian CD with a choir director whose maiden surname was Zorych.

He knew our family's history and recognised the unusual surname, linking it to the family who had escaped. The CD came with an email address for the choir's administrator and a picture of my sister, Kvitka, the choir's conductor. The picture confirmed the young man's suspicions. My sister looked remarkably like his grandmother.

An email was sent to the choir's administrator in Toronto, who then forwarded it to my sister. In the fall of 2015, my phone rang. My sister was calling to tell me a most astonishing story. It was that my father's family, whom we had presumed dead, was alive and had found us here in Canada. Imagine the shock of finding out members of my father's family existed and still lived near Mostyska.

We received a very long and detailed email from the grandson, who gave us a history of what had happened to the members of the family.

Hard to believe that after more than seventy years, we discovered they were alive. We promised to visit them the following spring. Four of us made arrangements to fly to Ukraine—me, my sister, and our daughters, Rayisa, and Zoja.

We had a problem. The family in Ukraine wanted the four of us to stay with them in their home. Having visited Ukraine and knowing how tight the living quarters were, we tried to decline the offer. It wasn't easy. We knew they would try to pay for our hotel rooms. Somehow, this had to be resolved. That was my job.

The question was how not to insult the family. My pitch was that we were elderly and needed the privacy and easy access to a washroom. I had had surgery and I was up at least twice during the night—I did not wish to disturb anyone. Besides, we were financially comfortable and our daughters were even better off than we were. (I employed a little white lie in order to make this work.) Our host and his wife had good jobs, but their money did not stretch to entertaining unknown new family members. The couple had two young children and could not afford their own house. They lived with her parents.

We certainly made the right decision. Knowing Ukrainian hospitality, I knew they would give up their bedrooms and sleep on the floor. We did not wish for that to happen.

We began our trip in Kyiv. I wanted Zoja to see the magnificent city that was nearly two thousand years old. I had been to Kyiv twice before, once in 1991 and again in 2007.

In 1991, Ukraine obtained its independence. Kyiv was a mess. Everything needed fixing. Hot water was a luxury. As I walked around the city, I saw the workers busy fixing up the churches and heritage sites. I asked them why they were working on churches when people had difficulty getting hot water. Their reply was simple. The churches and the buildings were the country's heritage—their national pride was far more important than hot water.

In 1991, there had been only a few places to buy food. I stood and watched the food queues grow outside the shops. People lined up and waited for the doors to open at 11 a.m. to buy what they could afford. Elderly people emerged with purchases of bread and cheese and immediately sat down on the stairs to eat. They were hungry. I found this disturbing. I walked into the market building to take a look. It was not a well-stocked place, and what there was, was very expensive. Butter was ten dollars a pound, equivalent to a month's salary for a doctor. Butter was a luxury few could afford.

A lot of buying occurred on the black market. Even professionals were selling items on the black market to make ends meet. I met a few doctors who were busy trying to supplement their incomes. Inflation was incredibly high.

However, there was one high-end market in the middle of Kyiv where one could buy sturgeon black caviar for two dollars in a small tin. Tourists were buying, but not the locals. Local folks were not seen there.

In 1994, when I was in Lviv with my mother, the cost of living had improved. One could afford bread, cheese—maybe even a sausage. My mother and I took some friends to the newly established gelato kiosk. This was so exciting for our friends. Now, gelato flavours were available in the main square in Lviv on a daily basis. An unheard of luxury.

Thirteen years later, in 2007, when I was back in Kyiv, there were restaurants and grocery stores where one could buy almost anything The prices were high, but far more reasonable than they had been in 1991. In 2007, particularly in Kyiv, it was difficult to talk to store clerks or waiters in Ukrainian, because they pretended not to understand. Independence had still not penetrated their consciousness. Perhaps they were nervous, because

use of the Ukrainian language was still considered to be risky, like it had been during the Soviet period.

In 2018, when I took my husband to Ukraine, I felt the country had changed. People believed they were living in an independent, democratic, and free nation. It felt good to be able to speak to people and order in restaurants using our native language.

In 2016, when my sister and I first met our father's closest relatives, we were driven to Yevstakhiia's little house, in a village about five kilometres from Mostyska. We sat on a bench in her backyard and talked and talked. As my cousin talked, I realised the land and everything on it was sacred to the people. Yevstakhiia liked to sit on her back stoop and look at her garden, her flowers, her chickens, and the majestic storks that feed in her fields. All of this provided her with a unique brand of luxury.

There were four rooms in Yevstakhiia's tiny house. The kitchen was part of the hallway. We took a tour of her house after she had served us a meal. The food she placed on the table came from her own garden. She had grown everything we ate, and it was all very good. There were copious dishes—mostly salads and preserves. The dessert table had almost as many dishes as the main meal. In the summer, she used her summer kitchen to cook, bake, marinate, and preserve. The summer kitchen and the chicken coop were two connected sheds, separate from the house.

I had looked at her kitchen located in the hallway and noticed a small gas burner, a cupboard that looked like a hutch with a small surface on which to prepare the dishes, and a table on which the prepared dishes were placed. I did not see a sink, so I blurted out, "But where is your sink?"

"I have a sink, right here in the bathroom, just a few steps from my kitchen. How many sinks do you think I need?!"

She put me in my place. If she knew that most of us in North America have a sink or two in the kitchen and one in the bathroom, she would consider that kind of excess frivolous. I said no more.

I did not see a fridge. I'm sure there was a cold-storage cellar under the house. She was content and happy. Why would it be otherwise?

We sat on the back stoop and looked at her pristine garden, her fruit trees, and her row of very tall and magnificent lilac trees—and there, in the front yard, stood a tall post where a pair of storks had built a huge nest. The storks swooped around her garden and, as we watched them, we were filled with admiration and wonder. Yevstakhiia is right—her life is splendid.

What I want to acknowledge, one more time, is my father's family's graciousness. During our 2016 visit, they were thrilled to meet my sister, me, and our daughters. We were the daughters and granddaughters of the man who had indirectly been responsible for their exile to Siberia, yet they treated us with such warmth and excitement and took us around to meet the few remaining family members who lived in Mostyska. We toured and took in the sights. Then, they arranged a private session in the small town museum, where the grandson pointed to the wall of heroes and said, "These are our heroes. We will remember them, always."

A partial photo of the wall of heroes in Mostyska, which is dedicated to those who fought for an independent and democratic Ukraine. My father is included here, in the middle of the top row.

My Mother's Wisdom

My mother dispensed bits of wisdom. Here are two such bits, which I have enjoyed sharing with friends who knew her—and even those who didn't.

Her first piece of advice when I left home was:

> You will know what people think of you by the way they serve you coffee. If they produce a freshly brewed cup, then you are indeed a valued guest. If they pour a cup from the bottom of the coffee pot, then you know you are considered only as a tolerated guest. If, however, they offer you a reheated cup of coffee—never, never go back.

Her second piece of advice concerned the effort I put into entertaining my friends. It was bewildering to my mother. She would point out to me that this was Canada, and none of my friends were starving. So why did I make such a fuss over meal preparations?

I asked her, "Well how do you entertain your friends?" "Well," she answered, "My friends come to talk to me to have a spirited conversation. I put out a good box of chocolates, a bottle of wine, and a lovely rose in a vase to produce an aesthetically pleasant environment. And then, we talk."

Remembering My Father

My father was an eccentric, funny, and very principled man. I have already described his love of pranks and his friendly torture of my prospective beaux. We knew he would die for a democratic, free Ukraine. He loved company and loved to chat and reminisce about the happy times in Ukraine.

He also loved this vast country, Canada, and when he acquired a car, a splendid dark green Desoto, we drove to different destinations on weekend excursions, just to have a look and enjoy the countryside. My father was a good driver, though he went a bit too fast at times. I don't think he ever had an accident, though.

As we continued to prosper, my father obtained a very good job selling policies for a Ukrainian insurance company. It was called the Ukrainian National Association, and it had headquarters in New Jersey. I often drove with him to the Catskill Mountains in New York State, where the company had a resort and where most of his business meetings were held. It was easy for me to pass the time with other kids at the resort, and we played tennis, swam, and hiked while our parents were otherwise engaged. I loved those road trips, just my father and I, singing all the way to the resort, then all the way back to Toronto.

He spoiled me. Often, he took me to New York for an afternoon and gave me a handful of paper dollars to spend at Macy's Department Store. I was in high school, and in those days, it was pretty safe to leave a teenager alone in the city for a couple of hours while attending to some business elsewhere in the city. We arranged a pickup time at a specific corner. I would be there, waiting, when our car turned the corner and my dad would pick me up.

As a child, I knew very little about his time as a Resistance participant. It was not something he talked about when we children were around. The little bits and pieces I remember hearing, I have scattered throughout this book. I guess the thing I remember most about him was his generosity, his humour, and his ability to question my Latin language skills. Most of all, I remember his passion for Ukrainian folksongs, which we sang constantly on our long trips, rarely repeating a song.

I am so grateful for those memories.

My Children's Memories

Zoja's Story

Let me start by saying that when we were young, my sisters and I played a lot of sports. We were incredibly active and almost always hungry. So, we could eat. Almost anytime. Almost everything.

When I was still in elementary school, my parents went overseas for something—a vacation or as observers of an election, I can't be sure—our grandmother came down from Toronto to stay with us for a week. We were a bit apprehensive, as my mom is a great cook, but my grandmother ... well, she could make a few great dishes, but "cook" isn't the first word that comes to mind when we remember her.

We came home from school the first day and, boy, were we pleased. Waiting for us in the kitchen were fried pork chops, potatoes, and, likely, bread. It was glorious. My parents commuted an hour to and from work, so they were never home when we got off the bus. Even if they were, pork chops as an after-school snack was not in the cards. We devoured our after-school snack. Happy and carefree, we all went our respective ways—to read, watch TV, or play outside. Who can remember the minutiae of everyday life?

What I do remember is that snack. And, about an hour and a half later, being called down for dinner. Despite her wicked sense of humour—and she did have a great sense of humour, albeit one married with a fierce presence and stubborn personality—food was no joke. We tried to reason with her— she had literally just served us a full meal for a snack, we couldn't possibly be hungry. She rejected this claim. She was told to provide an afternoon snack, which she did. And she had been told to feed us dinner, which she was hellbent on doing.

We were still full, and it didn't matter. We were going to eat again, whether or not we liked it, needed it, or wanted it. This was not an argument the three of us could win. Thankfully, our bottomless pit-for-stomachs and a general disregard for the food supply in our home paid off under normal circumstances. The three of us looked at each other, then simply tucked in for dinner number two. I remember being uncomfortably full. If memory serves, I also remember an unstated agreement among us three to avoid the kitchen after school for the remainder of the week.

Larissa's Story

My grandmother never learned that much English, and I only learned a bit of Ukrainian. As a result, we often did things that required little conversation: learning embroidery, going for walks, hunting for mushrooms, posing for pictures in front of flower gardens with our shirts buttoned up to our chins and our skirts hiked up, and making varenyky (potato dumplings). There are only a few Ukrainian phrases I can say without hesitation. Things like "Good day!"; "You have really nice hair"; "Hungry?"; "I like chocolate"; and "I don't understand". And like these phrases, there are memories that come quickly, almost on command.

Mamo was visiting us in small-town Ontario, where she discovered Canadian mint ice cream bars. These were ice cream popsicles that had a solid chocolate slab in the middle, covered with mint ice cream, then dipped in chocolate, for a fantastic experience of sweet delight. She fell head over heels in love with them and would buy packages of these on each subsequent visit, as, apparently, they were not available in Toronto. She saved a box and asked the manager of the grocery store in Prescott how she could get them in Toronto. The manager of the store was completely confused by the request, and my grandmother was unsatisfied with his lack of information. I can only imagine the reaction when she returned to Toronto, went to her grocery store, and presented the manager there with an empty box of ice cream bars followed by an interrogation as to why they were not available to her there.

Ham. She always arrived with a small ham tucked in her luggage, and insisted that we take one home with us after every visit to Toronto. It never made sense, yet these small hams would get packed up and lugged hundreds of kilometres from Toronto to wherever we were living.

We would often help her make varenyky when she visited us. Once, as we sat there pinching together the edges of the dough, she looked at my work and said, "Those are not beautiful. Who would eat such varenyky?" When I replied that I would, she did not look pleased, but we continued our work.

I still make varenyky from time to time, and enjoy the repetition of folding and pinching together dough over spoonfuls of mashed potatoes. My varenyky are still not beautiful, but they are delicious, so I eat them and share them—and sometimes a story or two—with my friends.

Kvitka's Story

I feel very blessed to have had as much time with my grandmother, Mamo, as I did. I was thirty-six when she passed away. She saw my growth from a precocious youngster to a mature woman … hopefully! She met my husband, Nick, when we were first dating. I have so many memories of her throughout my life. My grandmother would only speak to me in Ukrainian, refusing to speak in English—and only if she really had to. So, I developed an ear for Mamo's Ukrainian. It was amusing when she would get annoyed with her friends for speaking to me in English when she felt I should be able to understand them in Ukrainian—which, unfortunately for them, I often did not. In a way, Mamo and I developed our own language. My grandfather, Dido, had passed away before I became a teenager, but I was fortunate to have spent many summers as a young child with both my grandparents, either in Toronto or at their cottage on Mary Lake.

I remember Dido to be a kind man with a great sense of humour and a deep laugh. He didn't speak much English, so our conversations were always in Ukrainian—broken Ukrainian at best. One of our favourite things to do together was to watch cop shows on TV, because it wasn't that difficult to understand what was happening. The plot was almost always the same; something bad happened, the police would have to investigate, and by the end of the show, the mystery would be solved and the criminal would be apprehended.

One afternoon, I remember hanging out with Dido at the house on Leland Avenue when the doorbell rang. I peered through the semi-opaque windows on the front door and could see that there was a police officer standing there. I ran to get my grandfather, wondering why the police would be there, and called out "Dido, Police! Police!" He misunderstood me, and walked into the living room and sat down on the sofa to turn on the TV. I had to pull him to the front door and point to the police officer before he realised what was going on. We had a good chuckle when we re-enacted the story for Mamo.

Many people who knew Mamo have humorous stories to share, because she was quite a character, with a quick wit and a biting tongue in any language. Yet my most vivid memories of her are not funny. They consist of small moments—a look she gave when she wanted me to do something for her, the gleam in her eye when she was telling me a story, the sound of her laugh as she talked with one of her friends on the phone, or the nightly rituals we had when I stayed with my grandparents as a kid.

I think those rituals are what I remember most. I often shared a bed with Mamo at the cottage or slept on the sofa at the house. Each night, she would bring a washcloth and wipe my feet before tucking me under the covers. We would chat about our day, and Mamo would softly sing little songs to me. The one I remember best was one that started with ""Котику, Котику, де ти бував? Що ти чував?" Loosely translated, it means "kitty cat, kitty cat, where have you been? What have you heard?" And finally, she would tell me in Ukrainian that "the moon is sleeping, the forest is sleeping, the animals are sleeping, and now, Kvitochko, you are sleeping." She would then turn off the lights and I would go to sleep. I miss those moments. I miss her.

Correspondence:
Imprisoned Women
Writers and Artists

When I went through my mother's papers, there were some letters relating to the dismal state of Ukrainian women political prisoners. I was unaware of this correspondence. The letters were fragile, the writing tight and very small. Space mattered, as paper was precious and hard to come by during the Soviet period.

After my mother's funeral, her shoebox of tightly packed letters was lost. However, we knew the prisoners who did return to Ukraine came home sick and weak, and some came back as invalids.

In 1977, a book was published in North America about Ukrainian imprisoned women writers. My mother was involved in the publishing of *Invincible Spirit: Art and Poetry of Ukrainian Women Political Prisoners in the USSR*. This book was published to alert the Western world to the horrific plight of Ukrainian women prisoners. The women were imprisoned for their vocal nationalist opinions as described in their writing, their poems, and even their embroidery, which has been part of the evolution of Ukrainian culture since prehistoric times.

Ukrainian embroidery was an important factor in the national rebirth that the 19th century brought to Ukraine: along with the Ukrainian language and song, Ukrainian embroidery nourished the national consciousness of the Ukrainian masses.[6]

I love the art of Ukrainian embroidery. I do a little—not very well. I enjoy the work—the focus of it and the evolving pattern as I stitch. I make bookmarks, much like the women who stitched their work in prison—often on small pieces of cloth, even though essential things like thread and needles were not easily available.

A human being in prison is a human being who is of necessity inventive. Thread was obtained [by the women political prisoners] from sacks and coloured dyes extracted from plants. Needles were fashioned from sharpened bits of wire. And thus was embroidery produced in prison stealthily, away from the eyes of the guards, and obviously marked with a large measure of artistic individualism. Again, it became a symbol. But this time not as an invitation of happiness, nor as a statement of national feeling, but as a symbol of [the] national dignity of the suffering Ukrainian political prisoner.[7]

It is hard to believe people were imprisoned "merely for having embroidered articles in their possession, articles which advertised this national consciousness."[8]

It is incredible that political women prisoners took huge risks and continued to write and embroider. There were harsh consequences for any artistic expression that symbolised the existing injustices. The arts awakened a desire for an independent and free Ukraine; the release of all political prisoners; and promoted respect for and adherence to human rights. The prisoners' artistic

---

6   Lidia Burachynska, "Symbolism in Ukrainian Embroidery Art," in *Invincible Spirit: Art and Poetry of Ukrainian Women Political Prisoners in the USSR,* ed. Bohdan Arey (Baltimore: Smoloskyp, 1977), 11.

7   Burachynskà, "Symbolism," p.12.

8   Burachynska, "Symbolism," 11.

efforts and political sentiments made them vulnerable to intimidation, repression, physical and sexual assault. Despite the horrendous consequences the women prisoners did not stop their crusade for justice.

From the book Invincible Spirit, I have chosen two women prisoners to highlight the cruelty of their plight. Iryna Senyk and Oksana Popovych were both arrested in 1944 and sentenced to ten years in camp No. 3 in Mordovia in Siberia. These were very young women—Iryna was twenty-one and Oksana was eighteen. Both returned home after that internment as invalids, unable to walk without crutches.

In 1972, over a hundred Ukrainian dissidents had been arrested and were awaiting sentencing. Iryna Senyk was one of them. Sentenced a year later to six years of hard labour for her "collection of poetry in which she expressed her Ukrainian patriotism, for her defence of Ukrainian political prisoners, and for her acquaintance with several families of the Ukrainian civil and national rights movement."[9]

Here is one of her poems, translated by Bohdan Yasen:

Outside, it's spring. It's May.
Everything is in bloom.
But in my heart a restless sadness
has blossomed blue—a periwinkle.
Yes, yes.
Longing is a constant of my life.
Longing for what was lost …
Or perhaps, longing for what was never found.[10]

A fragment of a letter by Iryna Senyk reads: "May violets of the heart bloom even in the raging killer frost."[11]

---

9   Bohdan Arey, "Biographies", in *Invincible Spirit: Art and Poetry of Ukrainian Women Political Prisoners in the USSR* (Baltimore: Smoloskyp, 1977), 88.

10 Iryna Senyk, trans. Bohden Yasen, in *Invincible Spirit: Art and Poetry of Ukrainian Women Political Prisoners in the USSR* (Baltimore: Smoloskyp, 1977), 81.

11 Iryna Senyk, "Letter fragment", trans. Bohden Yasen, in *Invincible Spirit: Art and Poetry of Ukrainian Women Political Prisoners in the USSR* (Baltimore: Smoloskyp, 1977), 74.

An incredibly strong woman, Iryna Senyk knew that "for every word she spoke in defence of imprisoned Ukrainian patriots, she would have to pay with long years of imprisonment. But can a person remain indifferent to the fate of those who want to live a life of freedom?"[12]

СІМ ДОЛЕЙ

Українська Гельсінська Група

9 листопада 1976 року у Києві, наперекір усім перешкодам та помимо великої небезпеки, була створена Українська Гельсінська Група. Їх було 47 осіб: 45 громадян України, 2 громадяни Росії. На чолі з письменником Миколою Руденком, з такими членами, як В'ячеслав Чорновіл, Левко Лук'яненко, Михайло Горинь, Василь Стус та інші. Вони — об'єднані ідеєю самостійности України, створили непередбачену комуністичним режимом епоху безстрашности, вільної думки, державницьких вимог.

Їх БУЛО 47... 10 членів-засновників, до яких приєдналося ще 37 членів. Поміж ними було сім жінок. Всі вони стали борцями за ідею, яка внесла зміни в історію України, поставила її незалежною на мапі світу.

Сім жінок. Сім долей. Сім прикладів самопожертви для нас усіх, для нашого покоління і майбутніх поколінь.

У 1979 році написане звернення "Лямєнтація" до урядів і громадськости вільного світу: Українська Гельсінська Група втрачає можливість існування. Москва не відважилася її формально зліквідувати, але руками КГБ внарештувала по черзі її членів, приписуючи їм видумані кримінальні злочини... "Лямєнтацію" підписали Оксана Мешко, Ніна Строката та Ірина Сеник...

Згадаймо ж їх усіх 47-ох, а головно тих сімох мужніх жінок, для яких доля України була більш важлива, ніж власне життя чи спокійне проживання у неволі.

ОКСАНА МЕШКО — народилася 30 січня 1905 р. Політичний в'язень в роках 1947-1955. Засуджена в 1981 році на 6 місяців психіятричного ув'язнення та 5 років заслання. Померла 2 січня 1991 року. Член-засновник УГГ.

НІНА СТРОКАТА-КАРАВАНСЬКА — народилася 31 січня 1926 р., політичний в'язень у 1971-1974 роках. Померла 2 серпня 1998 р. в Америці. Член-засновник УГГ.

ОЛЬГА ГЕЙКО-МАТУСЕВИЧ — народилася 9 вересня 1953 р., політичний в'язень у роках 1980-1983. В 1983 році знову засуджена на три роки ув'язнення.

ОКСАНА ПОПОВИЧ — народилася 2 лютого 1926 р., політичний в'язень у роках 1944-1954, засуджена в 1975 році на 8 років ув'язнення та 5 років заслання.

ІРИНА СЕНИК — народилася 8 червня 1926 р., політичний в'язень у роках 1944-1954 та 1972-1981. В 1998 році Ірина Сеник, номінована СФУЖО, була вибрана американським "Рочестерським Комітетом 100 героїнь" однією із ста героїнь світу з-поміж 3,000 кандидаток з 71-ої країни.

СТЕФАНІЯ ШАБАТУРА — народилася 6 листопада 1938 р., політичний в'язень у роках 1972-1980. Маємо героїчних жінок, маємо ким гордитися, маємо з кого брати приклад посвяти в нашому щоденному житті.

НАДІЯ СВІТЛИЧНА — народилася 8 листопада 1936 р., політичний в'язень у 1972-1976 роках, тепер мешкає в Америці. Доба дії Української Гельсінської Групи вимагає широкого дослідження для історії. Їхня відвага, самопосвята та віра у майбутнє України хай будуть прикладом для нас та майбутніх поколінь.

С.О.

14

"ЖІНОЧИЙ СВІТ" СІЧЕНЬ-БЕРЕЗЕНЬ 2003

Seven women belonged to the Ukrainian Helsinki Group, a group of forty-five dissidents. Between 1976 and 1988, the ten creators of the Ukrainian Helsinki Group were hunted, and imprisoned, exiled, or placed in mental institutions. The five women belonging to the Helsinki Group are mentioned in the book Invincible Spirit. They are marked here with a small check on the left of their photo.[13]

---

12   Bohdan Arey, "Biographies," in *Invincible Spirit: Art and Poetry of Ukrainian Women Political Prisoners in the USSR* (Baltimore: Smoloskyp, 1977), 103.

13   "Ukrainian Helsinki Group," *Ukrainian Woman's World 54, no. 11 (2003), 14.*

Oksana Popovych was arrested a second time in 1975, as the world celebrated International Women's Year. Her sentence was eight years of a hard labour camp and five years of exile from Ukraine. Her crime the second time was for helping the families of political prisoners.

> She knew what it meant to be a prisoner, cast into a subterranean cell, behind iron bars or barbed wire, to be remembered. One is revived then, knowing that the struggle was not in vain. Someone thinks about you. Someone is continuing what you could not finish.[14]

She was sentenced just before she was scheduled to undergo a series of operations to enable her to walk without crutches. At her sentencing, she was heavily guarded: "Where could she escape to? But that was not what the almighty judges feared. It was before her spirit that they trembled."[15]

I don't know where one gets the courage to confront an evil force and know that there will be no understanding, no mercy, no justice. What could a poem that pays tribute to one's land, culture, and traditions do to ignite such hatred? Yet there are, among us, people with an incredible force of conviction, ones that stand for human decency regardless of the consequences.

* * *

Unfortunately, not all of my mother's friends had lives with happy endings in Canada. She had a friend who had been a dancer in Ukraine. She was very beautiful, with jet-black hair and amazing blue eyes. She taught us ballet. We loved her. She moved with such grace, and as a teacher, she convinced us we were made for a life on the stage.

She also was a fine musician, and came to our house because there was a piano in the dining room. Dancing or playing the piano seemed to give her the will to go on. Also, I think she genuinely liked us children, simply because we liked her and made no demands on her.

---

14 Bohdan Arey, "Biographies," in *Invincible Spirit: Art and Poetry of Ukrainian Women Political Prisoners in the USSR* (Baltimore: Smoloskyp, 1977), 107.

15 Bohdan Arey, "Biographies," in *Invincible Spirit: Art and Poetry of Ukrainian Women Political Prisoners in the USSR* (Baltimore: Smoloskyp, 1977), 107.

She often played the piano for us. The music was haunting and sad. She was sad. She often cried as she played, and I could not understand why such a beautiful and talented woman could be so unhappy.

At times, I could overhear her conversation with my mother. She kept asking if my mother had heard if anyone knew of her fiancé's whereabouts. Somewhere during their exodus, they were separated, and she never found him. She was devastated. Eventually, she started to lose weight. She believed he had been tortured, and that now they were coming for her.

She started to suspect her friends. She still came to visit us, but she stopped accepting the food we offered. She claimed my mother would not know if the food on her plate was poisoned. They, the enemy, were clever, and she believed that she had to be most vigilant. So my mother gave her boiled eggs, which she accepted for a short time. Then, she stopped eating altogether. She simply lost the will to live.

Ukrainians who lived through the war came to Canada seemingly able to cope with day-to-day life. Most did, but there were some who did not. Some could not reconcile with what they had lost, and although Canada provided freedom, wars can destroy people's faith in humanity and compromise their will to live.

Whether these people ended up in institutions depended a lot on who kept an eye on them. In Canada, there were resources available for families and the community to access for those traumatised by the war. These folks coped quite well, until events like thunderstorms unsettled them. They would hide, and someone would try to find them and convince them the war was over.

As my mother grew older, she grew very concerned about being deported. She did not want me to reveal our real surname to anyone. At first, it was to protect the family left in Ukraine—then, later on in her life, it became an unreasonable fear. I found it so difficult to observe my mother—this brilliant, well-read, quick-tongued woman, develop an obsession with safety. I guess it never really leaves you, the uncertainty and the fear that you could lose your freedom—even in Canada.

She was not the only one with this worry hanging over her head. Other ageing friends were haunted by their narrow escape to freedom. This evolved slowly as the years added up. The reality of what had happened brought on a new fear—the fear that all could be lost—your safety and your freedom gone before you could peacefully move into your next life.

Despite the worry that inched itself into her life, my mother was an extraordinary person. She lived a very productive and fulfilling life. She devoted endless hours to her causes and volunteer work. Everything was considered important—obligations that had to be fulfilled.

Though she was a force to be reckoned with, she had compassion. She had a soft spot for anyone who needed help. Because she was so well connected to the Ukrainian community, she knew which organisation to tap for assistance with housing, employment, or other issues. After all, she had been involved with most of them. At her funeral, when people came to celebrate her life, they said, "Your mother was amazing. She worked constantly for the good of the community, and she helped many people." One person, my mother's friend, said with a smile, "She stood out, lecturing us about community first—not our personal self. Did you know she even arranged a couple of marriages? Who would have guessed that? I bet you didn't!"

My mother being honoured for her work.

This blouse is typical of the ornate embroidery found in Northeastern Carpathian Mountains. The necklace holds strands of antique coral beads, often worn as part of a traditional regional costume, throughout Ukraine.

My mother and Olha Malanchuk had a solid friendship throughout their lives in Canada. They shared laughs and causes with equal commitment and passion.

Olha's portrait by Borys Plaksiy, a distinguished Ukrainian artist from Cherkasy Region in Central Ukraine. This is a wonderful painting of a sophisticated, gracious intellectual. I have such happy memories of spending time with her.

My father's choir in Ukraine—no one would be out of tune. If they were, he would hear them. My sister also has that talent—she hears everything when she directs her choir.

Yaroslava Zorych, February 17, 1917–November 2, 2009
Bohdan Zorych, August 30, 1912–March 12, 1984

Bibliography

Arey, Bohdan. Invincible Spirit: Art and Poetry of Ukrainian Women Political Prisoners in the USSR. Baltimore: Smoloskyp, 1977.

Burachynska, Lidia. "Symbolism in Ukrainian Embroidery Art." In Invincible Spirit: Art and Poetry of Ukrainian Women Political Prisoners in the USSR, edited by Bohdan Arey, 11. Baltimore: Smoloskyp, 1977.

Darewych, Daria. Myron Levytsky. Toronto: Ukrainian Artists' Association, 1985.

Grundland, Fritz. This is Canada: Songbook with Sheet Music for Voice and Piano with Chords. Toronto: Gordon V. Thompson, 1967.

Martyn, Bohdan. Mostyska and Mostyshyna: From the Earliest Times to the 21st Century. Mostyska, Ukraine: Bohdan Martyn, 2009.

Senyk, Iryna. Translated by Bohden Yasen. In Invincible Spirit: Art and Poetry of Ukrainian Women Political Prisoners in the USSR, edited by Bohdan Arey, 81. Baltimore: Smoloskyp, 1977.

Shevchenko Scientific Society. Ukraine: A Concise Encyclopaedia. Toronto: University of Toronto Press, 1971.

"Ukrainian Helsinki Group." Ukrainian Woman's World 54, no. 11 (2003), 14.

Ukrainian Woman's World vol. 54, no. 12 (2003), cover art.

About the Author

Chrystyna Zorych Holman is a Ukrainian-Canadian immigrant, author, teacher, mother, and wife. Originally from Mostyska, Ukraine, her family would make the difficult crossing of the Atlantic to flee political strife in their native land as part of a wave of immigration to Canada post-WWII, where her family would go on to build a life—first in Manitoba, then Toronto. Having lived through dramatic circumstances leaving their homeland and establishing life anew, Chrystyna long wished to collect her family's story in one chronicle—for her sake, that of her children, and that of anyone interested in the Ukrainian diaspora in Canada.

Besides having lived through these experiences firsthand, Chrystyna's background as a teacher of students young and old—including teaching newcomers English—has given her a deep appreciation for the multicultural and ethnic fabric of Canadian society and the many ways people come to be part of it. She has travelled all over the world—including to Australia, Japan, Ukraine, and China—as part of her teaching work. She holds a Master's Degree in Education.

Chrystyna lives in Charlottetown, Prince Edward Island with her husband, Alan, and their frisky, energetic Scottie. Together, they have three daughters, who live in Ontario and Quebec, and two beautiful grandsons. Beyond writing, Chrystyna loves to read, travel, host, and cook—and learn anything new.

Printed in Canada